Good Housekeeping

one-dish
meals

The Good Housekeeping Triple-Test Promise

 We make sure that every recipe that bears the **Good Housekeeping** name works in any oven, with any brand of ingredient, no matter what. That's why, in our test kitchens at the **Good Housekeeping Research Institute,** we test each recipe at least three times—and, often, several more times after that.

When a recipe is first developed one member of our team prepares the dish and we judge it on these criteria: It must be **delicious, family-friendly, healthy,** and **easy to make.**

1. The recipe is then tested several times to fine-tune the flavor and ease of preparation, always by the same team member, using the same equipment.

2. Next, another team member follows the recipe as written, **varying the brands of ingredients and kinds of equipment.** Even the types of stoves we use are changed.

3. A third team member repeats the whole process **using yet another set of equipment and alternative ingredients.**

By the time our recipes appear on these pages, they are guaranteed to work in any kitchen, including yours. WE PROMISE.

Good Housekeeping

one-dish
meals

100 DELICIOUS RECIPES

HEARST BOOKS
A division of Sterling Publishing Co., Inc.

New York / London
www.sterlingpublishing.com

Rosemary Ellis	Editor in Chief
Susan Westmoreland	Food Director
Susan Deborah Goldsmith	Associate Food Director
Delia Hammock	Nutrition Director
Sharon Franke	Food Appliances Director
Richard Eisenberg	Special Projects Director

Supplemental Text by Anne Wright
Book design by Richard Oriolo

The Library of Congress has cataloged the
original edition of this title as:
Good Housekeeping : 100 best one dish
recipes.
　　p. cm.
1. Entrees (Cookery) 2. Casserole
cookery. I. Good Housekeeping
Institute (New York, N.Y.)
　TX740.G55 2003
　641.8'2--dc21

　　　　　　　　　　　　　2003001536

10　9　8　7　6　5　4　3　2　1

Published by Hearst Books
A Division of Sterling Publishing
Company, Inc.
387 Park Avenue South,
New York, NY 10016

Good Housekeeping and Hearst Books
are trademarks of
Hearst Communications, Inc.

The Good Housekeeping Cookbook Seal
guarantees that the recipes in this
cookbook meet the strict standards of the
Good Housekeeping Research Institute, a
source of reliable information and a
consumer advocate since 1900. Every
recipe has been triple-tested for ease,
reliability, and great taste.

www.goodhousekeeping.com

Distributed in Canada by
Sterling Publishing
℅ Canadian Manda Group,
165 Dufferin Street
Toronto, Ontario, Canada M6K 3H6
Distributed in Australia by Capricorn Link
(Australia) Pty. Ltd.
P.O. Box 704, Windsor, NSW 2756
Australia

All rights reserved.
Manufactured in China

Sterling ISBN-13: 978-1-58816-738-5
　　　ISBN-10: 1-58816-738-0

Contents

Foreword

Everyone loves one-dish meals, and no wonder. What could be better than breaking the crust of a potpie brimming with gravy and chunks of meat? Or digging into a plate piled high with succulent stir-fried shrimp and juicy vegetables?

Now we've compiled our 100 all-time favorite recipes—the ones readers and staff ask for time and time again—into this one volume, so you can enjoy the very best of our one-dish meals.

What do all these dishes have in common? Each one is a complete meal on its own—streamlining menu planning, shopping, cooking, and cleanup.

This comprehensive collection offers many different types of one-dish meals—quick-cooking pastas, stews, down-home potpies, Asian-inspired stir-fries, hearty sandwiches, and a wealth of crowd-pleasing casseroles. You're sure to find the perfect fit for every occasion.

In winter, when the gang's been out sledding and skiing, serve up Polenta and Sausage Casserole, an Italian specialty that's sure to stick to their ribs. In spring, why not showcase fresh seasonal vegetables in one of our easy stir-fries, such as Thai Chicken with Asparagus?

Our cool, crisp salads make for satisfying warm-weather eating, from old favorites such as Niçoise Salad to great new ideas like Couscous and Smoked-Turkey Salad. On a cool, crisp autumn afternoon what could be better for a tailgate party than Chili Potpie with Cheddar-Biscuit Crust?

With the growing interest in healthy eating in mind, we've included many low-fat recipes. We also lightened up old favorites like Chicken Shepherd's Pie, trimming fat and calories but not flavor. You'll also find some wonderfully hearty meatless dishes such as Penne with Three Cheeses and Porcini Mushrooms and Vegetarian Black Bean Burritos.

While one-dish meals make great everyday fare, they are also ideal for entertaining. Why not try our Couscous Paella, Shrimp Creole, or Carbonnades à la Flamande for your next company dinner?

But the best part of this book—we think—is that every recipe has been triple-tested in the Good Housekeeping kitchens to ensure great results every time you make it. So get ready to treat your friends and family to some wonderful eating—any time of the year.

Susan Westmoreland
FOOD DIRECTOR, GOOD HOUSEKEEPING

A Great Start

When you need dinner in a hurry, canned chicken and vegetable broth make it easy, and all of the recipes in this book will taste delicious made with broth right off your pantry shelves. But if you want a truly superlative meal, nothing beats the flavor of homemade broth. And, it's easy to make. Start the broth on a day when you have time to let it simmer for four hours. Be sure to plan your menu ahead to use the cooked chicken in a soup, sandwich, or salad. Our recipes yield fairly large amounts, which means you can freeze the broth in sturdy containers for up to three months, and it will be on hand when you need it—almost as easy as canned!

Homemade Chicken Broth

PREP 10 minutes plus cooling   **COOK** 4 hours 30 minutes   **MAKES** 5–6 cups

In 6-quart saucepot, combine **1 chicken (3 to 3½ pounds), including neck** (giblets reserved for another use), **2 carrots,** peeled and cut into 2-inch pieces, **1 stalk celery,** cut into 2-inch pieces, **1 medium onion,** cut into quarters, **5 parsley sprigs, 1 garlic clove,** ½ **teaspoon dried thyme,** ½ **bay leaf,** and enough **water** to cover **(about 3 quarts)**; heat to boiling over high heat. Skim foam from surface. Reduce heat and simmer 1 hour, turning chicken once and skimming. Remove from heat; transfer chicken to large bowl. When cool enough to handle, remove skin and bones from chicken. (Reserve chicken for another use.) Return skin and bones to saucepot and heat to boiling. Skim foam; reduce heat and simmer 3

Skimming chicken broth.

hours. Strain broth through colander into large bowl; discard solids. Strain again through sieve into containers; cool. Cover and refrigerate to use within 3 days, or freeze up to 4 months. To use, skim and discard fat from surface of broth.

Three Bean Vegetarian Chili
(see page 48)

EACH CUP About 36 calories | 3 g protein | 4 g carbohydrate | 1 g total fat (1 g saturated) | 3 mg cholesterol | 91 mg sodium.

Vegetable Broth

PREP 25 minutes **COOK** 2 hours **MAKES** about 6 cups

Cut off roots and trim dark green tops from **4 large leeks**; thinly slice leeks. Rinse leeks in large bowl of cold water, swishing to remove sand; transfer to colander to drain, leaving sand in bottom of bowl. In 6-quart saucepot, combine leeks, **2 to 4 garlic cloves,** not peeled, **1 cup water,** and **pinch salt**; heat to boiling. Reduce heat to medium; cover and cook until leeks are tender, about 15 minutes. Add **1 large all-purpose potato,** peeled, cut lengthwise in half, and thinly sliced, **1 small fennel bulb,** trimmed and chopped (optional), **3 parsnips,** peeled and thinly sliced (optional), **2 large carrots,** peeled and thinly sliced, **3 stalks celery with leaves,** thinly sliced, **4 ounces mushrooms,** trimmed and thinly sliced, **10 parsley sprigs, 4 thyme sprigs**, **2 bay leaves, 1 teaspoon whole black peppercorns,** and **12 cups water**; heat to boiling. Reduce heat and simmer, uncovered, at least 1 hour 30 minutes. Taste and continue cooking if flavor is not concentrated enough. Season with **salt and pepper** to taste. Strain broth through fine-mesh sieve into containers, pressing on solids with back of wooden spoon to extract liquid; cool. Cover and refrigerate to use within 3 days, or freeze up to 4 months.

EACH CUP About 19 calories | 1 g protein | 4 g carbohydrate | 0 g total fat (0 g saturated) | 0 mg cholesterol | 9 mg sodium.

Better Beans

Dried beans that have been soaked and cooked are tastier than canned and yield a firmer texture. Plus, they are much lower in sodium.

Before soaking, sort through the beans to remove tiny stones or debris. Place the beans in a colander and rinse well with cold water, running your fingers through the beans to reveal any bits of dirt. Transfer the beans to a large bowl. (Dried beans rehydrate to at least double their size, so be sure to use a large bowl.) Add enough cold water to cover the beans by two inches. The standard "overnight" (about eight hours) soaking time is really for the cook's convenience. The job is done when the beans have swelled to about double their size, which takes about four hours, but beans can be soaked for up to twenty-four hours. In hot weather, to prevent the beans from fermenting, refrigerate them while they soak. If you want to reduce the soaking time by about half, cover the beans with boiling water instead of cold. Just before cooking, drain the soaked beans and rinse them again. Discard the soaking water and cook the beans in fresh water.

Quick-Soak Technique

When time is of the essence, use this fast method: Combine the beans and cold water in a pot and heat to boiling; cook for three minutes. Remove from the heat, cover tightly, and set aside for one hour; drain and rinse the beans. Although this process saves time, quick-soaked beans tend to break up during cooking. In a chili or bean stew, a few broken beans are not a problem. But if you want the beans to remain whole, for a bean salad, for example, use the long-soak method.

Cooking Dried Beans

There is an enormous range of cooking times for dried beans. Use the directions on the package as a guide, then taste often to check for doneness, because their age and relative dryness will affect the exact time.

Dried beans should always be cooked in soft water, or they will be tough. If you live in an area with hard water, add a pinch of baking soda to the cooking water. Because water boils at a lower temperature in high altitudes, beans will take longer to cook at high altitudes; be sure they are well-soaked and softened before cooking. Adding salt to beans at the beginning of cooking toughens the skin and increases the cooking time. However, beans usually taste better when seasoned early, so we often use a minimal amount of salt when the cooking begins, then add the remainder at the end.

Although the volume changes slightly with each bean variety, one cup dried beans averages two cups cooked beans. Large beans, like limas, yield about two and one-half cups, whereas small beans, such as black beans, yield just under two cups.

Ready to Go

For the best flavor we like to cook from scratch when possible. Fresh shrimp and mussels are more succulent than frozen. However, they must be properly prepared before you add them to your recipe. Here's how to do so quickly and easily. Be sure to use fresh seafood within two days of purchase.

Shelling and Deveining Shrimp

1. With kitchen shears or a small knife, cut the shrimp shell along the outer curve, just deep enough into the flesh to expose the dark vein.

2. Peel back the shell from the cut and gently separate the shell from the shrimp. Discard the shell (or use it to make fish stock).

3. Remove the vein with the tip of a small knife and discard. Rinse the shrimp under cold running water.

Scrubbing and Debearding Mussels

Scrub mussels well under cold running water. To debeard, grasp the hairlike beard with your thumb and forefinger and pull it away, or scrape it off with a knife. (Cultivated mussels usually do not have beards.)

Soups & Stews

Seafood Stew
recipe on page 46

Boeuf Bourguignon

Americans have come to love this French classic. It originated in the Burgundy region, which is renowned for the wonderful wine that is the basis for this robust stew. Serve with boiled potatoes or chunks of crusty French bread.

PREP 30 minutes   **COOK** 2 hours 45 minutes   **MAKES** 6 main-dish servings

2 slices bacon, chopped

2 pounds lean boneless beef chuck, trimmed and cut into 1½-inch pieces

2 teaspoons vegetable oil

1 large onion (12 ounces), chopped

2 carrots, peeled and chopped

2 garlic cloves, finely chopped

2 tablespoons all-purpose flour

2 teaspoons tomato paste

2 cups dry red wine

½ bay leaf

1 teaspoon plus pinch salt

¼ teaspoon plus pinch ground black pepper

1 pound small white onions, peeled

3 tablespoons butter or margarine

1 teaspoon sugar

1 cup water

1 pound mushrooms, trimmed and cut into quarters if large

1. In nonreactive 5-quart Dutch oven, cook bacon over medium heat until just beginning to brown. With slotted spoon, transfer bacon to medium bowl.

2. Pat beef dry with paper towels. Add 1 teaspoon oil to Dutch oven and increase heat to medium-high. Add beef, in batches, to bacon drippings and cook until well browned, using slotted spoon to transfer beef as it is browned to bowl with bacon. Add remaining 1 teaspoon oil if necessary.

3. Reduce heat to medium. Add chopped onion, carrots, and garlic to Dutch oven; cook until onion and carrots are tender, about 8 minutes. Stir in flour; cook 1 minute. Stir in tomato paste; cook 1 minute. Add wine, bay leaf, 1 teaspoon salt, and ¼ teaspoon pepper, stirring until browned bits are loosened. Return beef and bacon to Dutch oven; heat to boiling. Reduce heat; cover and simmer until beef is very tender, about 1 hour 30 minutes. Remove bay leaf. Skim and discard fat.

4. Meanwhile, in 10-inch skillet, combine small white onions, 1 table-spoon butter, sugar, and water. Heat to boiling; cover and simmer until onions are just tender, about 10 minutes. Remove cover and cook over medium-high heat, swirling pan occasionally, until water has evaporated and onions are golden. Transfer to bowl; keep warm.

5. In same skillet, melt remaining 2 tablespoons butter over medium-high heat. Add mushrooms and remaining pinch each salt and pepper; cook, stirring, until mushrooms are tender and liquid has evaporated. Stir onions and mushrooms into stew.

EACH SERVING About 415 calories | 33 g protein | 20 g carbohydrate | 23 g total fat (9 g saturated) | 116 mg cholesterol | 261 mg sodium.

Beef and Barley Soup

Nutty-tasting barley is often paired with lamb, but we found it tastes great when teamed up with beef. What's more, barley is rich in fiber, B vitamins, and minerals. Serve with a salad to round out the meal.

PREP 45 minutes   **COOK** 2 hours 30 minutes
MAKES about 16 cups or 8 main-dish servings

1 tablespoon plus 4 teaspoons vegetable oil

3 medium stalks celery, diced

1 large onion, diced

1½ pounds boneless beef chuck, cut into ½-inch pieces

½ teaspoon salt

2 cans (13¾ to 14½ ounces each) beef broth

1 can (14½ ounces) diced tomatoes

6 cups water

1 cup pearl barley

5 medium carrots (12 ounces), peeled and cut crosswise into ¼-inch-thick slices

5 medium parsnips (12 ounces), peeled and cut crosswise into ¼-inch-thick slices

2 medium turnips (8 ounces), peeled and diced

3 strips (3" by 1" each) orange peel

pinch ground cloves

1. In 8-quart Dutch oven, heat 1 tablespoon vegetable oil over medium-high heat until hot. Add celery and onion and cook until tender and golden, about 10 minutes, stirring occasionally; transfer vegetables to bowl.

2. Pat beef dry with paper towels. In same Dutch oven, heat 2 teaspoons oil over high heat until hot. Add half of beef and cook until browned on all sides. Remove to plate. Repeat with the remaining 2 teaspoons oil and the beef.

3. Return beef to Dutch oven. Stir in salt, celery mixture, beef broth, tomatoes with their juice, and water; heat to boiling over high heat. Reduce heat to low; cover and simmer 1 hour.

4. Add barley, carrots, parsnips, turnips, orange peel, and cloves; heat to boiling over high heat. Reduce heat to low; cover and simmer 50 to 60 minutes, until beef, barley, and vegetables are tender.

EACH SERVING About 320 calories | 25 g protein | 36 g carbohydrate | 9 g total fat (3 g saturated) | 41 mg cholesterol | 740 mg sodium.

Chinese-Spiced Beef Stew

Our new beef stew with broccoli and snow peas has a thin yet flavorful sauce accented with ginger and star anise. Try it over linguine or Chinese egg noodles.

🕐 **PREP** 30 minutes **COOK** 2 hours to 2 hours **MAKES** 8 main-dish servings

2 pounds boneless beef chuck, cut into 1½-inch pieces

2 tablespoons vegetable oil

⅓ cup dry sherry

2 tablespoons sugar

3 tablespoons soy sauce

1 piece fresh ginger (3" by 1"), peeled and thinly sliced

2 garlic cloves, peeled

2 whole star anise

4 strips (3" by 1" each) orange peel

3 cups water

1 bunch broccoli (1½ pounds), cut into 1½" by 1" pieces

4 ounces snow peas, trimmed

1 bunch green onions, cut into 2-inch pieces

1. Pat beef dry with paper towels. In 5-quart Dutch oven, heat 1 tablespoon vegetable oil over medium-high heat until hot. Add half of beef and cook until browned on all sides. Transfer beef to plate. Repeat with remaining oil and beef.

2. Return beef to Dutch oven. Add sherry, sugar, soy sauce, ginger, garlic, star anise, orange peel, and water; heat to boiling over high heat. Reduce heat to low; cover and simmer 1 to 1½ hours, until the meat is fork-tender.

3. With slotted spoon, transfer meat to serving bowl and keep warm. Discard star anise. Increase heat to high and boil liquid 15 minutes or until reduced to about 2 cups. Skim off fat from surface.

4. Meanwhile, in a 4-quart saucepan, heat *1 inch water* to boiling over high heat. Add broccoli. Reduce heat to low; cover and simmer 5 minutes. Add snow peas and green onions and cook, covered, about 3 minutes longer or until all vegetables are tender-crisp. Drain vegetables and add to beef mixture. Pour reduced broth on top.

EACH SERVING About 370 calories | 27 g protein | 12 g carbohydrate | 24 g total fat (8 g saturated) | 85 mg cholesterol | 460 mg sodium.

Spanish Beef Stew

Unlike most stews, this one starts with a whole piece of meat, which is shredded after cooking. A vibrant mix of bell peppers, chiles, and cinnamon gives it a distinctive flavor. Serve over rice, if you like.

PREP 45 minutes   **COOK** 3 hours 30 minutes   **MAKES** 6 main-dish servings

I beef flank steak (1¾ pounds)

I medium onion, coarsely chopped

I medium carrot, coarsely chopped

I bay leaf

2 teaspoons salt

5 cups water

4 teaspoons olive oil

I large onion, sliced

I red pepper, cut into ½-inch strips

I yellow pepper, cut into ½-inch strips

I green pepper, cut into ½-inch strips

3 garlic cloves, crushed with garlic press

3 serrano or jalapeño chiles, seeded and minced

¼ teaspoon ground cinnamon

I can (14½ to 16 ounces) tomatoes

capers for garnish

1. Cut flank steak into thirds. In 5-quart Dutch oven, heat steak, chopped onion, carrot, bay leaf, 1 teaspoon salt, and water to boiling over high heat. Reduce heat to low; cover and simmer 2½ to 3 hours, until meat is very tender. Remove Dutch oven from heat and let steak stand, uncovered, 30 minutes. (Or, cover and refrigerate overnight.)

2. In 12-inch skillet, heat olive oil over medium-high heat. Add sliced onion, peppers, and remaining 1 teaspoon salt and cook, stirring often, 15 minutes or until vegetables are tender. Stir in garlic, chiles, and cinnamon and cook 30 seconds. Stir in tomatoes with their juice; cook 5 minutes.

3. Remove beef to bowl; strain broth. Reserve 2 cups broth. (Reserve remaining broth for use another day.) With 2 forks, shred beef into fine strips.

4. Stir reserved 2 cups broth and shredded meat into pepper mixture and simmer, uncovered, stirring occasionally, 10 minutes. Sprinkle with capers to serve.

EACH SERVING About 350 calories | 38 g protein | 10 g carbohydrate | 17 g total fat (7 g saturated) | 65 mg cholesterol | 720 mg sodium.

Super Bowl Chili

Our recipe for Texas-style chili contains small *chunks* of beef rather than ground. The classic version doesn't contain beans, but we replaced a portion of the meat with red kidney beans to cut some fat. Serve with corn bread or tortilla chips.

PREP 30 minutes   **COOK** about 2 hours   **MAKES** 14 cups or 12 main-dish servings

2 tablespoons olive oil

2 pounds boneless beef for stew, cut into 1/2-inch chunks

4 garlic cloves, crushed with garlic press

2 red peppers, cut into 1/2-inch dice

2 jalapeño chiles, seeded and minced

1 large onion, chopped

1/3 cup chili powder

2 cans (28 ounces each) whole tomatoes in puree

1 can (6 ounces) tomato paste

1/4 cup sugar

2 teaspoons salt

2 teaspoons dried oregano

2 cups water

2 cans (15 to 19 ounces each) red kidney beans, rinsed and drained

1. In 8-quart saucepot or Dutch oven, heat 1 teaspoon oil over high heat until hot. Add one-third of beef and cook until browned on all sides and liquid evaporates, 6 to 8 minutes, stirring often. With slotted spoon, transfer beef to bowl. Repeat with remaining beef, using 1 teaspoon oil per batch; set beef aside.

2. Add remaining 1 tablespoon oil to drippings in saucepot and heat over medium-high heat until hot. Stir in garlic, red peppers, jalapeños, and onion; cook until vegetables are tender, about 10 minutes, stirring occasionally. Stir in chili powder; cook 1 minute.

3. Return beef to saucepot. Stir in tomatoes with their puree, tomato paste, sugar, salt, oregano, and water, breaking up tomatoes with side of spoon; heat to boiling over high heat. Reduce heat to low; cover and simmer 1 hour and 30 minutes. Stir in beans and cook 10 to 30 minutes longer or until meat is fork-tender, stirring occasionally.

EACH SERVING About 275 calories | **25 g protein** | **30 g carbohydrate** | **7 g total fat (2 g saturated)** | **36 mg cholesterol** | **1,115 mg sodium.**

Two-Alarm Chili

A little cocoa powder helps balance the seasonings in this meaty chili. If you like really hot chili, increase the pickled jalapeño and ground red pepper to taste.

PREP 20 minutes   **COOK** 35 minutes   **MAKES** 6 main-dish servings

I tablespoon olive oil

I medium onion, chopped

2 garlic cloves, finely chopped

2 green peppers, chopped

2 pounds ground beef chuck

3 pickled jalapeño chiles, seeded and finely chopped (2 tablespoons)

3 tablespoons chili powder

2 teaspoons unsweetened cocoa

1¼ teaspoons salt

¾ teaspoon ground coriander

½ teaspoon dried oregano

¼ teaspoon ground red pepper (cayenne)

I can (14 to 16 ounces) tomatoes, chopped

1. In nonstick 12-inch skillet, heat oil over medium heat. Add onion and garlic and cook, stirring occasionally, until onion is tender, about 5 minutes. Add green peppers and cook, stirring, until tender-crisp, about 5 minutes longer.

2. Add ground beef and cook, breaking up meat with side of spoon, until meat is no longer pink. Stir in pickled jalapeños, chili powder, cocoa, salt, coriander, oregano, and ground red pepper and cook 1 minute. Add tomatoes with their juice and heat to boiling. Reduce heat and simmer chili, stirring occasionally, until slightly thickened, 15 to 20 minutes longer.

EACH SERVING About 326 calories | 33 g protein | 10 g carbohydrate | 18 g total fat (6 g saturated) | 94 mg cholesterol | 758 mg sodium.

GH Test Kitchen Tip

For extra flavor and fun, offer an assortment of toppings such as grated Cheddar, chopped black olives, diced avocado, and sour cream.

Latin American Pork Stew

Pork, black beans, cilantro, and sweet potatoes give this dish authentic Latino flavor.

🕐 **PREP** 30 minutes **BAKE** 1 hour 30 minutes
MAKES about 10 cups or 8 main-dish servings

2 teaspoons olive oil

2 pounds boneless pork loin, cut into 1-inch pieces

1 large onion, chopped

4 garlic cloves, minced

1 can (14½ ounces) diced tomatoes

1 cup loosely packed fresh cilantro leaves and stems, chopped

1 teaspoon ground cumin

¾ teaspoon salt

½ teaspoon ground coriander

¼ teaspoon ground red pepper (cayenne)

2 cups water

3 medium sweet potatoes (1½ pounds), peeled and cut into ½-inch chunks

2 cans (15 to 19 ounces each) black beans, rinsed and drained

1. Preheat oven to 350°F. In nonstick 5-quart Dutch oven, heat olive oil over medium-high heat. Add pork in batches and cook until lightly browned, about 5 minutes per batch. Transfer pork to medium bowl.

2. Reduce heat to medium. In drippings in Dutch oven, cook onion until tender, about 10 minutes, stirring frequently. Add garlic and cook 1 minute longer.

3. Add tomatoes with their juice, cilantro, cumin, salt, coriander, ground red pepper, and water; heat to boiling over high heat. Stir in pork; cover and bake 30 minutes.

4. Stir in sweet potatoes; cover and bake 40 minutes longer or until meat and sweet potatoes are very tender. Stir in black beans; cover and bake 15 minutes longer or until heated through.

EACH SERVING About 340 calories | 36 g protein | 36 g carbohydrate | 9 g total fat (3 g saturated) | 58 mg cholesterol | 735 mg sodium.

Roasted Chile and Tomatillo Stew

At New Mexico's chile stands, green chile is as popular as red. Tangy tomatillos, which look like small, firm green tomatoes covered with papery husks, are sold fresh or canned. Dark green poblano chiles are sometimes called fresh ancho chiles, but don't confuse them with dried anchos.

PREP 1 hour **BAKE** 2 hours 30 minutes **MAKES** 8 main-dish servings

4 poblano chiles or 2 green peppers

1 bunch cilantro

3 garlic cloves, minced

1½ teaspoons salt

2 pounds boneless pork shoulder, cut into ¾-inch pieces

2 medium onions, finely chopped

3 serrano or jalapeño chiles, seeded and minced

1 teaspoon ground cumin

¼ teaspoon ground red pepper (cayenne)

2 pounds tomatillos, husked, rinsed, and each cut into quarters

1 can (15¼ to 16 ounces) whole-kernel corn, drained

warm flour tortillas (optional)

1. Preheat broiler. Line broiling pan (without rack) with foil. Place poblanos or green peppers in pan and broil at closest position to source of heat, turning occasionally, until charred all over, about 15 minutes. Wrap foil around poblanos and allow to steam until cool enough to handle. Remove and discard skin and seeds; cut poblano chiles into 1-inch pieces.

2. Turn oven control to 325°F. Chop enough cilantro leaves and stems to measure ¼ cup; chop and reserve another ¼ cup cilantro leaves for garnish. On cutting board, mash garlic to a paste with salt. Transfer garlic mixture to heavy 5-quart Dutch oven with cilantro leaves and stems, pork, onions, serranos, cumin, and ground red pepper. Toss to combine. Cover and bake 1 hour.

3. Stir in tomatillos and roasted poblanos. Cover and bake 1½ to 2 hours longer, until meat is very tender. Skim fat. Stir in corn; heat through. Sprinkle with reserved cilantro and serve with tortillas if you like.

EACH SERVING WITHOUT TORTILLAS About 370 calories | 23 g protein | 20 g carbohydrate | 23 g total fat (8 g saturated) | 67 mg cholesterol | 600 mg sodium.

Moroccan-Style Lamb with Couscous

This sweet but slightly spicy stew is served on a bed of couscous, which, like Italian pasta, is made from semolina wheat.

PREP 20 minutes **COOK** 1 hour 45 minutes **MAKES** 8 main-dish servings

2 pounds boneless lamb shoulder, trimmed and cut into 1¼-inch pieces

2 tablespoons olive oil

2 garlic cloves, finely chopped

1½ teaspoons ground cumin

1½ teaspoons ground coriander

1 large onion (12 ounces), cut into 8 wedges

1 can (14½ to 16 ounces) stewed tomatoes

1 cinnamon stick (3 inches)

1¼ teaspoons salt

¼ teaspoon ground red pepper (cayenne)

1 cup water

2 pounds sweet potatoes (3 large), peeled and cut into 2-inch pieces

2 cups couscous (Moroccan pasta)

1 can (15 to 19 ounces) garbanzo beans, rinsed and drained

1 cup dark seedless raisins

¼ cup chopped fresh cilantro

1. Pat lamb dry with paper towels. In non-reactive 5-quart Dutch oven, heat 1 tablespoon oil over medium-high heat until very hot. Add half of lamb and cook until browned, using slotted spoon to transfer meat to bowl as it is browned. Repeat with the remaining 1 tablespoon oil and the remaining lamb.

2. To drippings in Dutch oven, add garlic, cumin, and coriander; cook 30 seconds. Return lamb to Dutch oven. Stir in onion, tomatoes, cinnamon stick, salt, ground red pepper, and water; heat to boiling over high heat. Reduce heat; cover and simmer, stirring occasionally, 45 minutes. Stir in sweet potatoes; cover and simmer 30 minutes longer.

3. Meanwhile, prepare couscous as package label directs.

4. Add garbanzo beans and raisins to Dutch oven. Cover and cook, stirring once or twice, until lamb and vegetables are tender, about 5 minutes longer.

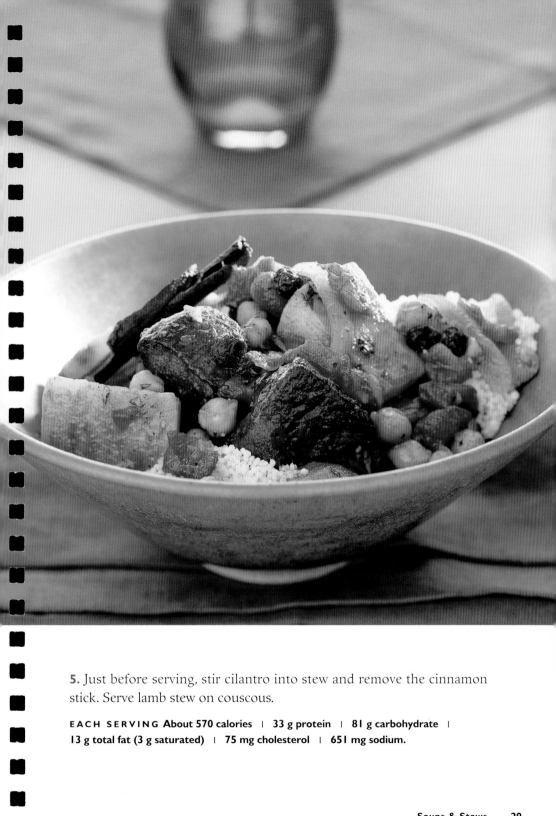

5. Just before serving, stir cilantro into stew and remove the cinnamon stick. Serve lamb stew on couscous.

EACH SERVING About 570 calories | 33 g protein | 81 g carbohydrate | 13 g total fat (3 g saturated) | 75 mg cholesterol | 651 mg sodium.

Moroccan-Style Chicken Stew

Our quick take on a Moroccan tagine—a sumptuous meat or poultry dish with spices, olives, and raisins—uses canned beans and chicken chunks to save time. Serve over white rice, if desired.

PREP 10 minutes   **COOK** 20 minutes   **MAKES** about 8 cups or 6 main-dish servings

1 tablespoon olive oil

1 medium onion, chopped

1 tablespoon all-purpose flour

1 teaspoon ground coriander

1 teaspoon ground cumin

½ teaspoon salt

¼ teaspoon ground red pepper (cayenne)

¼ teaspoon ground cinnamon

1½ pounds skinless, boneless chicken thighs, cut into 2-inch chunks

2 garlic cloves, crushed with garlic press

1 can (28 ounces) whole tomatoes in puree

1 can (15 to 19 ounces) garbanzo beans, rinsed and drained

⅓ cup dark seedless raisins

¼ cup salad olives (chopped pimiento-stuffed olives)

1 cup water

½ cup loosely packed fresh cilantro leaves

1. In nonstick 5- to 6-quart Dutch oven, heat oil over medium heat until hot. Add onion and cook 5 minutes or until light golden brown.

2. Meanwhile, in pie plate, mix flour with coriander, cumin, salt, ground red pepper, and cinnamon. Toss chicken with flour mixture to coat evenly.

3. Add chicken to Dutch oven and cook 7 minutes or until lightly browned, turning chicken over halfway through cooking time. Add garlic and cook 1 minute.

4. Stir in tomatoes with their puree, beans, raisins, olives, and water; simmer, uncovered, 5 minutes or until chicken is cooked through, breaking up tomatoes with side of spoon. Garnish with cilantro.

EACH SERVING About 305 calories | 29 g protein | 28 g carbohydrate | 9 g total fat (2 g saturated) | 94 mg cholesterol | 890 mg sodium.

Chicken and Sweet-Potato Stew

Coat chicken thighs with an exotic mix of cumin and cinnamon, then simmer with beta-carotene-rich sweet potatoes in a creamy peanut-butter sauce. Delectable over brown rice.

○ **PREP** 20 minutes **COOK** 45 minutes **MAKES** 4 main-dish servings

4 medium bone-in chicken thighs (about 1½ pounds), skin removed

1 teaspoon ground cumin

¼ teaspoon ground cinnamon

1 tablespoon olive oil

3 medium sweet potatoes (about 1½ pounds), peeled and cut into ½-inch chunks

1 medium onion, sliced

1 can (28 ounces) whole tomatoes in juice

3 tablespoons natural peanut butter

½ teaspoon salt

¼ teaspoon crushed red pepper

2 garlic cloves, peeled

¼ cup packed fresh cilantro leaves plus 2 tablespoons chopped cilantro leaves

1. Rub chicken thighs with cumin and cinnamon; set aside.

2. In nonstick 12-inch skillet, heat oil over medium heat. Add sweet potatoes and onion and cook until onion is tender, 12 to 15 minutes, stirring occasionally. Transfer sweet-potato mixture to plate.

3. Increase heat to medium-high. Add seasoned chicken, and cook 5 minutes or until chicken is lightly browned on both sides.

4. Meanwhile, drain tomatoes, reserving juice. Coarsely chop tomatoes and set aside. In blender at high speed or in food processor with knife blade attached, blend tomato juice, peanut butter, salt, crushed red pepper, garlic, and ¼ cup of the cilantro leaves until smooth.

5. Add sweet-potato mixture, peanut-butter sauce, and chopped tomatoes to skillet with chicken; heat to boiling over high heat. Reduce heat to low; cover and simmer 25 minutes or until juices run clear when chicken is pierced with tip of knife. To serve, sprinkle with chopped cilantro.

EACH SERVING About 410 calories | 26 g protein | 50 g carbohydrate | 12 g total fat (2 g saturated) | 76 mg cholesterol | 725 mg sodium.

Creole Chicken Gumbo

Gumbo gets much of its rich flavor from a deeply browned roux made with a generous amount of fat. Here, we've kept the same rich flavor but cut the fat by toasting the flour in the oven.

PREP 1 hour 10 minutes **COOK** 1 hour 30 minutes
MAKES 18 cups or 12 main-dish servings

⅔ cup all-purpose flour

12 large bone-in chicken thighs (about 3½ pounds), fat removed

12 ounces fully cooked andouille or kielbasa sausage, cut into ½-inch-thick slices

6 cups chicken broth

1 can (6 ounces) tomato paste

2 cups water

2 medium onions, thinly sliced

12 ounces okra, sliced, or 1 package (10 ounces) frozen cut okra, thawed

1 large yellow pepper, chopped

4 stalks celery with leaves, cut into ¼-inch-thick slices

¾ cup chopped fresh parsley

4 garlic cloves, thinly sliced

2 bay leaves

1½ teaspoons salt

1 teaspoon dried thyme

1 teaspoon ground red pepper (cayenne)

1 teaspoon ground black pepper

½ teaspoon ground allspice

1 can (14 to 16 ounces) tomatoes, drained and chopped

½ cup finely chopped green-onion tops

2 tablespoons distilled white vinegar

3 cups regular long-grain rice, cooked as label directs

1. Preheat oven to 375°F. Place flour in oven-safe 12-inch skillet. (If skillet is not oven-safe, wrap handle with double layer of foil.) Bake until flour begins to brown, about 25 minutes. Stir with wooden spoon, breaking up any lumps. Bake, stirring flour every 10 minutes, until it turns nut brown, about 35 minutes longer. Remove flour from oven and let cool. Strain flour through sieve to remove any lumps.

2. Heat nonreactive 8-quart Dutch oven over medium-high heat until very hot. Cook chicken, skin side down first, in batches, until golden brown, about 5 minutes per side. Transfer chicken pieces to large bowl as they are browned. Add sausage to Dutch oven and cook over medium heat, stirring constantly, until lightly browned, about 5 minutes. With slotted spoon, transfer sausage to bowl with chicken.

3. Reduce heat to medium-low. Gradually stir in browned flour, about 3 tablespoons at a time, and cook, stirring constantly, for 2 minutes.

4. Immediately add broth, stirring until browned bits are loosened from bottom of pan. Blend tomato paste with water and add to Dutch oven. Stir in onions, okra, yellow pepper, celery, ¼ cup parsley, garlic, bay leaves, salt, thyme, ground red pepper, black pepper, and allspice. Add sausage, chicken, and tomatoes; heat to boiling over high heat. Reduce heat and simmer until liquid has thickened, about 1 hour.

5. Add the remaining ½ cup parsley, green onions, and vinegar; heat through. Remove from heat; cover and let stand 10 minutes. Discard bay leaves. Serve gumbo in bowls over cooked rice.

EACH SERVING About 447 calories | 27 g protein | 28 g carbohydrate | 25 g total fat (8 g saturated) | 107 mg cholesterol | 1,357 mg sodium.

> ### GH Test Kitchen Tip
> This recipe makes a generous amount of gumbo. Any leftovers can be frozen.

Chicken with Rosemary Dumplings

It's not hard to cook melt-in-your-mouth dumplings. Just be sure that, during cooking, the pot stays covered and that the cooking liquid never exceeds a simmer. We used chicken breasts to shorten the prep and cooking time.

PREP 15 minutes **COOK** 1 hour **MAKES** 6 main-dish servings

2 tablespoons vegetable oil

6 large bone-in chicken-breast halves (3¼ pounds), skin removed

4 large carrots, peeled and cut into 1-inch pieces

2 large stalks celery, cut into ¼-inch-thick slices

1 medium onion, finely chopped

1 cup plus 2 tablespoons all-purpose flour

2 teaspoons baking powder

1½ teaspoons chopped fresh rosemary or ½ teaspoon dried rosemary, crumbled

1 teaspoon salt

1 large egg

1½ cups milk

2 cups water

1 can (14½ ounces) low-sodium chicken broth or 1¾ cups Chicken Broth (page 9)

¼ teaspoon ground black pepper

1 package (10 ounces) frozen peas

1. In 8-quart Dutch oven, heat 1 tablespoon oil over medium-high heat until very hot. Add 3 chicken-breast halves; cook until golden brown, about 5 minutes per side. With slotted spoon, transfer chicken pieces to bowl as they are browned. Repeat with remaining chicken.

2. Add remaining 1 tablespoon oil to drippings in Dutch oven. Add carrots, celery, and onion and cook, stirring frequently, until vegetables are golden brown and tender, about 10 minutes.

3. Meanwhile, prepare dumplings: In small bowl, combine 1 cup flour, baking powder, rosemary, and ½ teaspoon salt. In cup, with fork, beat egg with ½ cup milk. Stir egg mixture into flour mixture until just blended.

4. Return chicken to Dutch oven; add water, broth, pepper, and remaining ½ teaspoon salt. Heat to boiling over high heat. Drop dumpling mixture by rounded tablespoons on top of chicken and vegetables to make 12 dumplings. Reduce heat; cover and simmer 15 minutes.

5. With slotted spoon, transfer dumplings, chicken, and vegetables to serving bowl; keep warm. Reserve broth in Dutch oven.

6. In cup, blend remaining 2 tablespoons flour with remaining 1 cup milk until smooth; stir into broth mixture. Heat to boiling over high heat; boil 1 minute to thicken slightly. Add peas and heat through. Pour sauce over chicken and dumplings.

EACH SERVING About 437 calories | 46 g protein | 38 g carbohydrate | 10 g total fat (3 g saturated) | 137 mg cholesterol | 951 mg sodium.

Hearty Chicken and Vegetable Stew

A creamy sauce coats juicy chunks of chicken and a colorful array of vegetables in a dish that's pure comfort food.

PREP 45 minutes **COOK** I hour **MAKES** 4 main-dish servings

2 medium leeks (about 4 ounces each)

I fennel bulb (about I pound)

2 tablespoons olive oil

2 tablespoons butter or margarine

I pound skinless, boneless chicken-breast halves, cut into 1½-inch pieces

8 ounces mushrooms, thickly sliced

3 medium carrots (about 8 ounces), cut into 1-inch pieces

12 ounces red potatoes, cut into 1-inch pieces

I bay leaf

¼ teaspoon dried tarragon leaves

½ cup dry white wine

I can (14½ ounces) chicken broth

¼ cup water

¾ cup half-and-half or light cream

3 tablespoons all-purpose flour

I cup frozen peas, thawed

¾ teaspoon salt

1. Cut off roots and trim leaf ends of leeks; cut each leek lengthwise in half and separate leaves. Rinse well with cold running water to remove any sand. Cut leeks crosswise into ¾-inch pieces.

2. Cut root end and stalks from fennel bulb; discard. Cut the fennel bulb lengthwise into thin wedges.

3. In 5-quart Dutch oven or saucepot, heat 1 tablespoon olive oil over medium-high heat until hot. Add 1 tablespoon butter; melt. Add chicken and cook until chicken is golden and just loses its pink color throughout. With slotted spoon, transfer chicken to medium bowl.

4. To drippings in Dutch oven, add mushrooms and cook, stirring often, until golden (do not overbrown). Transfer mushrooms to bowl with chicken.

5. To Dutch oven, add remaining 1 tablespoon olive oil; heat until hot. Add remaining 1 tablespoon butter or margarine; melt. Add carrots, leeks,

fennel, potatoes, bay leaf, and tarragon. Cook vegetables 10 to 15 minutes, until fennel is translucent and leeks are wilted, stirring occasionally.

6. Add wine; cook 2 minutes, stirring. Add chicken broth and water; heat to boiling over high heat. Reduce heat to low; cover and simmer 20 minutes or until vegetables are tender.

7. In cup, mix half-and-half and flour until smooth. Stir half-and-half mixture into vegetable mixture; heat to boiling over high heat. Reduce heat to medium; cook 1 minute to thicken slightly. Stir in chicken, mushrooms, peas, and salt; heat through. Discard bay leaf.

EACH SERVING About 530 calories | **37 g protein** | **53 g carbohydrate** | **20 g total fat (5 g saturated)** | **85 mg cholesterol** | **985 mg sodium.**

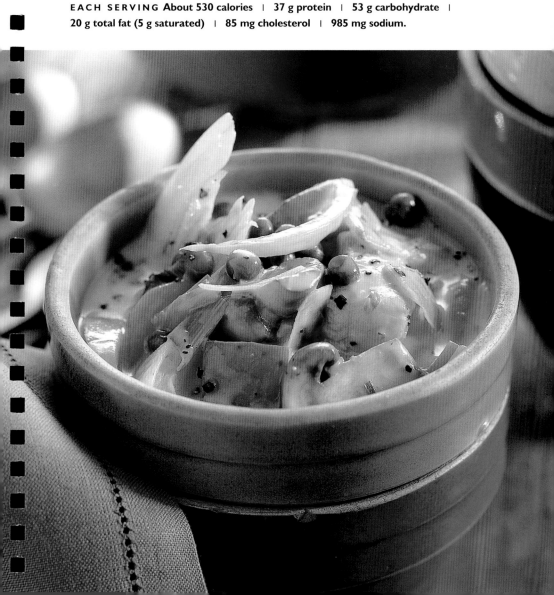

Coq au Vin

In this perennial French favorite, chicken cooks in a rich blend of red wine, brandy, herbs, and sautéed vegetables until tender and unbelievably delicious. Serve with boiled new potatoes or over rice or noodles.

PREP 30 minutes **COOK** 1 hour 45 minutes **MAKES** 8 main-dish servings

2 slices bacon (about 2 ounces), chopped

2 tablespoons olive oil

3 medium carrots, cut into ¼-inch dice

2 medium stalks celery, cut into ¼-inch dice

1 bag (16 ounces) frozen pearl onions, thawed

10 ounces large mushrooms, each cut into quarters

2 garlic cloves, minced

2 chickens (about 4 pounds each), each cut into 8 pieces, skin removed

3 tablespoons tomato paste

2 strips (3" by 1" each) fresh orange peel

3 tablespoons brandy

1¾ cups dry red wine

1 cup chicken broth

¾ teaspoon salt

¼ teaspoon coarsely ground black pepper

¼ teaspoon dried thyme

1 bay leaf

2 tablespoons all-purpose flour

3 tablespoons cold water

1. In 8-quart Dutch oven, cook bacon over medium heat until browned. With slotted spoon, transfer bacon to paper towels to drain. Pour off bacon fat from Dutch oven; reserve.

2. In same Dutch oven, heat 1 teaspoon bacon fat and 2 teaspoons oil until hot. Add carrots, celery, and pearl onions and cook, stirring occasionally, 20 minutes or until vegetables are tender and golden. Transfer vegetables to medium bowl.

3. In same Dutch oven, heat 2 teaspoons bacon fat and 1 teaspoon oil over medium-high heat until hot. Add mushrooms and cook 8 minutes or until tender and browned. Add garlic and cook 1 minute, stirring. Transfer mushrooms and garlic to bowl with other vegetables.

4. Add remaining 1 tablespoon oil to Dutch oven; add half of chicken pieces and cook over medium-high heat until browned; transfer to large bowl. Repeat with remaining chicken pieces.

5. Reduce heat to medium; add tomato paste and orange peel, and cook 30 seconds, stirring. (Tomato paste will stick to bottom of pan and darken, helping to intensify the flavor of the broth.) Add brandy and cook 30 seconds, stirring.

6. Return chicken pieces and vegetables to Dutch oven. Add wine, chicken broth, salt, pepper, thyme, and bay leaf; heat to boiling over high heat. Reduce heat to low; cover and simmer 30 minutes or until juices run clear when thickest part of chicken is pierced with tip of knife.

7. Meanwhile, in cup, with fork, mix flour with cold water until blended; set aside.

8. Transfer chicken to warm serving bowl. With slotted spoon, transfer vegetables to same bowl; cover and keep warm.

9. Slowly whisk flour mixture into broth in Dutch oven; heat until mixture boils and thickens slightly, stirring frequently. Spoon broth over chicken and vegetables in bowl. Discard bay leaf. Sprinkle with reserved bacon before serving.

EACH SERVING About 325 calories | **40 g protein** | **12 g carbohydrate** | **12 g total fat (3 g saturated)** | **122 mg cholesterol** | **485 mg sodium.**

Turkey Chili

This spicy potful is made with limas and white beans—just right for a simple Sunday-evening supper. Sprinkle each serving with crushed baked corn chips if you like.

PREP 20 minutes **COOK** 20 minutes **MAKES** about 6 cups or 4 main-dish servings

1 tablespoon olive oil

1 medium onion, chopped

3 garlic cloves, minced

1½ teaspoons chili powder

1 teaspoon ground cumin

1 teaspoon ground coriander

¼ teaspoon salt

¼ teaspoon coarsely ground black pepper

1 can (15 to 16 ounces) Great Northern or small white beans, rinsed and drained

1 can (14½ ounces) reduced-sodium chicken broth

1 package (10 ounces) frozen lima beans

1 can (4 to 4½ ounces) chopped mild green chiles

2 cups bite-size pieces leftover cooked turkey meat (about 8 ounces)

1 cup loosely packed fresh cilantro leaves, chopped

2 tablespoons fresh lime juice

lime wedges (optional)

1. In 5-quart Dutch oven, heat olive oil over medium heat until hot. Add onion and cook until tender, about 5 minutes, stirring often. Add garlic and cook 30 seconds. Stir in chili powder, cumin, coriander, salt, and pepper; cook 1 minute longer.

2. Meanwhile, in small bowl, mash half of Great Northern beans.

3. Add mashed beans and unmashed beans, chicken broth, frozen lima beans, green chiles, and turkey meat to mixture in Dutch oven. Heat to boiling over medium-high heat. Reduce heat to low; cover and simmer 5 minutes to blend flavors. Remove Dutch oven from heat; stir in cilantro and lime juice. Serve with lime wedges if you like.

EACH SERVING About 380 calories | 33 g protein | 45 g carbohydrate | 8 g total fat (2 g saturated) | 44 mg cholesterol | 995 mg sodium.

Poule au Pot with Tarragon

Stewed chicken and vegetables is a favorite Sunday supper in France. Use the leftover broth as the base for a soup.

🕐 **PREP** 15 minutes **COOK** 1 hour **MAKES** 4 main-dish servings

3 medium leeks (about 1 pound)

1 chicken (3½ pounds), cut into 8 pieces

1 pound small red potatoes

1 bag (16 ounces) carrots, peeled and cut into 3-inch pieces

4 cups water

1 can (14½ ounces) chicken broth or 1¾ cups Chicken Broth (page 9)

½ teaspoon salt

¼ teaspoon dried thyme

¼ teaspoon ground black pepper

1 large sprig plus 1 tablespoon chopped fresh tarragon

1. Cut off roots and trim dark green tops from leeks; cut each leek lengthwise in half, then crosswise into 3-inch pieces. Rinse in large bowl of cold water, swishing to remove sand; transfer to colander to drain, leaving sand in bottom of bowl.

2. In 6- to 8-quart Dutch oven, combine leeks, chicken, potatoes, carrots, water, broth, salt, thyme, pepper, and tarragon sprig. Heat to boiling over high heat. Reduce heat; cover and simmer until chicken loses its pink color throughout, about 45 minutes.

3. With slotted spoon, transfer chicken and vegetables to serving bowl. Remove and discard skin from chicken. Skim and discard fat from broth. Pour 1 cup broth over chicken. Refrigerate remaining broth for another use. To serve, sprinkle chopped tarragon on top.

EACH SERVING About 472 calories | 47 g protein | 44 g carbohydrate | 11 g total fat (3 g saturated) | 127 mg cholesterol | 859 mg sodium.

Peruvian Fisherman's Soup

A true treat for seafood lovers, this is more than just a soup. It's the main course and side dish all wrapped into one wonderfully flavorful meal in a bowl.

PREP 30 minutes **COOK** 25 minutes **MAKES** about 11 cups or 6 main-dish servings

1 tablespoon vegetable oil

1 medium onion, finely chopped

2 garlic cloves, minced

2 serrano or jalapeño chiles, seeded and minced

1 pound red potatoes, cut into ¾-inch chunks

3 bottles (8 ounces each) clam juice

¾ teaspoon salt

⅛ teaspoon dried thyme leaves

2 cups water

1 lime

1 pound monkfish, dark membrane removed, cut into 1-inch pieces

1 pound medium shrimp, shelled and deveined, leaving tail part of shell on if you like

¼ cup chopped fresh cilantro

1. In 4-quart saucepan, heat oil over medium heat until hot. Add onion and cook, stirring often, 10 minutes or until tender. Stir in garlic and chiles and cook 30 seconds. Add potatoes, clam juice, salt, thyme, and water; heat to boiling over high heat. Reduce heat to medium; cook 10 minutes.

2. Cut lime in half; cut half into wedges and set aside. Add other lime half and monkfish to soup; cover and cook 5 minutes. Stir in shrimp and cook 3 to 5 minutes longer, just until shrimp turn opaque throughout.

3. Remove lime half, squeezing juice into soup. Sprinkle soup with cilantro; serve with lime wedges.

EACH SERVING About 215 calories | 26 g protein | 16 g carbohydrate | 5 g total fat (1 g saturated) | 117 mg cholesterol | 640 mg sodium.

Creamy Italian White-Bean Soup

Canned beans make this Tuscan classic a snap to put together. Round out the meal with cheese and crusty bread.

PREP 15 minutes   **COOK** 40 minutes
MAKES about 6 cups or 4 main-dish servings

1 tablespoon vegetable oil

1 medium onion, finely chopped

1 medium celery stalk, finely chopped

1 garlic clove, minced

2 cans (15½ to 19 ounces each) white kidney beans (cannelloni), rinsed and drained

1 can (13¾ to 14 1/2 ounces) chicken broth

¼ teaspoon coarsely ground black pepper

⅛ teaspoon dried thyme leaves

1 bunch (10 to 12 ounces) spinach

1 tablespoon fresh lemon juice

freshly grated Parmesan cheese (optional)

1. In 3-quart saucepan, heat oil over medium heat until hot. Add onion and celery and cook 5 to 8 minutes, until tender, stirring occasionally. Add garlic; cook 30 seconds, stirring. Add beans, chicken broth, pepper, thyme, and 2 cups water; heat to boiling over high heat. Reduce heat to low; simmer, uncovered, 15 minutes.

2. Meanwhile, discard tough stems from spinach; thinly slice leaves.

3. With slotted spoon, remove 2 cups bean-and-vegetable mixture from soup; set aside. In blender at low speed, with center part of cover removed to allow steam to escape, blend remaining soup in small batches until smooth. Pour pureed into large bowl after each batch.

4. Return soup to saucepan; stir in reserved beans and vegetables. Heat to boiling over high heat, stirring occasionally. Stir in spinach and cook 1 minute or until wilted. Stir in lemon juice and remove from heat. Serve with Parmesan cheese if you like.

EACH SERVING WITHOUT PARMESAN CHEESE About 295 calories |
8 g protein | **46 g carbohydrate** | **5 g total fat (1 g saturated)** | **0 mg cholesterol** |
945 mg sodium.

Seafood Stew

A sumptuous mix of mussels, shrimp, and cod (see photo on page 15).

PREP 10 minutes   **COOK** 20 minutes   **MAKES** 4 main-dish servings

1¼ pounds all-purpose potatoes, peeled and cut into ½-inch pieces

1 can (14½ ounces) chunky tomatoes with olive oil, garlic, and spices

1 can (14½ ounces) chicken broth

16 large mussels, scrubbed and debearded (page 13)

16 large shrimp, shelled and deveined, with tail part of shell left on (page 13)

1 piece cod fillet (12 ounces), cut into 2-inch pieces

1 tablespoon chopped fresh parsley

1. In 2-quart saucepan, heat potatoes and *enough water to cover* to boiling over high heat. Reduce heat to low; cover and simmer 5 to 8 minutes, until potatoes are tender. Drain.

2. Meanwhile, in 5-quart Dutch oven, heat tomatoes with their liquid, chicken broth, and wine to boiling over high heat. Add mussels; reduce heat to medium. Cover and cook mussels 3 to 5 minutes, transferring mussels to bowl as shells open (see Tip).

3. Add shrimp and cod to Dutch oven; cover and cook 3 to 5 minutes, until shrimp and cod turn opaque throughout. Add potatoes and mussels; heat through. Sprinkle with chopped parsley.

EACH SERVING About 223 calories | 8 g protein | 39 g carbohydrate | 5 g total fat (0 g saturated) | 0 mg cholesterol | 790 mg sodium.

GH Test Kitchen Tip

Discard any mussels that have not opened after cooking.

Curried Vegetable Stew

Serve over white rice for an easy and delicious vegetarian meal. For extra crunch, add a sprinkling of toasted almonds.

PREP 15 minutes   **COOK** 25 minutes   **MAKES** 4 main-dish servings

2 teaspoons olive oil

1 large sweet potato (12 ounces), peeled and cut into ½-inch pieces

1 medium onion, cut into ½-inch pieces

1 medium zucchini (8 ounces), cut into 1-inch pieces

1 small green pepper, cut into ¾-inch pieces

1½ teaspoons curry powder

1 teaspoon ground cumin

1 can (15 to 19 ounces) garbanzo beans, rinsed and drained

1 can (14½ ounces) diced tomatoes

¾ cup vegetable broth

½ teaspoon salt

1. In deep nonstick 12-inch skillet, heat oil over medium-high heat. Add sweet potato, onion, zucchini, and green pepper; cook, stirring, until vegetables are tender, 8 to 10 minutes. Add curry powder and cumin; cook 1 minute.

2. Add garbanzo beans, tomatoes with their juice, broth, and salt; heat to boiling over high heat. Reduce heat to medium-low; cover skillet and simmer until vegetables are very tender but still hold their shape, about 10 minutes longer.

EACH SERVING About 223 calories | 8 g protein | 39 g carbohydrate | 5 g total fat (0 g saturated) | 0 mg cholesterol | 790 mg sodium.

GH Test Kitchen Tip

Curry powders can range from mild to hot—use whatever type you like best.

Three-Bean Vegetarian Chili

Hearty and colorful, this chili gets a wallop of flavor from a chipotle (smoked jalapeño) chile. If you can't find chipotles, add one or two additional fresh jalapeños, with seeds for more heat. Vary the beans according to what you have on hand, as long as you have 3 cups dried in all. Serve with corn bread or tortilla chips.

PREP 25 minutes plus soaking beans **COOK** 1 hour 45 minutes
MAKES about 10 cups or 6 main-dish servings

I cup dry white kidney beans (cannellini), soaked and drained (page 11)

I cup dry red kidney beans, soaked and drained (page 11)

I cup dry black beans, soaked and drained (page 11)

I tablespoon olive or vegetable oil

2 medium onions, chopped

3 carrots, peeled and chopped

I stalk celery, chopped

I red pepper, chopped

3 garlic cloves, finely chopped

I jalapeño chile, finely chopped

2 teaspoons ground cumin

½ teaspoon ground coriander

⅛ teaspoon ground cinnamon

⅛ teaspoon ground red pepper (cayenne)

I can (28 ounces) tomatoes in puree

I chipotle chile in adobo (see Tip, page 158), finely chopped, or I teaspoon ground chipotle chile

2 teaspoons salt

¼ teaspoon dried oregano

2 cups water

I package (10 ounces) frozen whole-kernel corn, thawed

½ cup chopped fresh cilantro

1. In nonreactive 5-quart Dutch oven, combine white kidney, red kidney, and black beans and *enough water to cover by 2 inches*; heat to boiling over high heat. Reduce heat; cover and simmer until beans are tender, about 1 hour. Drain beans and return to Dutch oven.

2. Meanwhile, in nonstick 10-inch skillet, heat oil over medium heat. Add onions, carrots, celery, and red pepper. Cook, stirring frequently, until carrots are tender, about   10 minutes. Stir in garlic, jalapeño, cumin, coriander, cinnamon, and ground red pepper; cook 30 seconds. Stir in tomatoes with their puree, chipotle chile, salt, and oregano, breaking up tomatoes with side of spoon. Heat to boiling; reduce heat and simmer 10 minutes, stirring several times.

3. Add tomato mixture and water to beans in Dutch oven; heat to boiling over medium-high heat. Reduce heat; cover and simmer, stirring occasionally, 15 minutes. Stir in corn and cook 5 minutes longer. Remove from heat and stir in ¼ cup cilantro. Spoon chili into bowls and sprinkle with remaining ¼ cup cilantro.

EACH SERVING About 461 calories | **25 g protein** | **86 g carbohydrate** |
4 g total fat (1 g saturated) | **0 mg cholesterol** | **1,048 mg sodium.**

Tuscan Vegetable Soup

Healthy and hearty—dust with freshly grated Parmesan cheese.

PREP 45 minutes plus soaking beans   **COOK** 1 hour 30 minutes
MAKES about 14 cups or 6 main-dish servings

5 medium carrots

1 jumbo onion (1 pound)

8 ounces dry Great Northern beans
(1⅓ cups), soaked and drained
(page 11)

1 bay leaf

3 tablespoons olive oil

4 ounces pancetta or cooked ham,
chopped

3 large stalks celery, coarsely chopped

1 fennel bulb (1 pound), trimmed
and coarsely chopped

2 garlic cloves, finely chopped

2 cans (13¾ to 14½ ounces each)
chicken broth

1 pound all-purpose potatoes (about
3 medium), peeled and cut into
½-inch pieces

1 medium head escarole (about
12 ounces), cut crosswise into
¼-inch-wide strips

½ teaspoon salt

grated Parmesan cheese (optional)

1. Cut 1 carrot crosswise in half. Coarsely chop remaining carrots; set aside. Cut onion into 4 wedges. Leave 1 wedge whole; coarsely chop remaining wedges.

2. In 4-quart saucepan, heat beans, carrot halves, onion wedge, bay leaf, and *6 cups water* to boiling over high heat. Reduce heat to low; cover and simmer 40 minutes to 1 hour, until beans are tender, stirring occasionally. Drain beans and vegetables, reserving *3 cups cooking liquid*. Discard carrot halves and onion wedge.

3. In 5-quart saucepot or Dutch oven, heat olive oil over medium-high heat. Add pancetta, celery, fennel, coarsely chopped carrot, and coarsely chopped onion; cook 15 minutes or until vegetables begin to brown, stirring occasionally. Add garlic; cook for 1 minute, stirring.

4. Stir in chicken broth, cooked beans, reserved 3 cups bean cooking liquid, potatoes, and escarole; heat to boiling over high heat. Reduce heat to low; cover and simmer 15 to 20 minutes, until all vegetables are very tender. Discard bay leaf. Stir in salt. Serve with grated Parmesan cheese if you like.

**EACH SERVING WITHOUT PARMESAN CHEESE About 335 calories |
17 g protein | 48 g carbohydrate | 10 g total fat (2 g saturated) |
18 mg cholesterol | 935 mg sodium.**

Casseroles & Oven Dishes

**Lamb Shanks with
White Beans and Roasted Endive
recipe on page 54**

Carbonnades à la Flamande

This Belgian standard makes a hearty cold-weather dinner. It should be prepared with a full-flavored dark beer to complement the sweet onions. But in a pinch, use lager. Serve over egg noodles.

◔ PREP 45 minutes COOK 2 hours 30 minutes MAKES 8 main-dish servings

3 tablespoons olive or vegetable oil

2 pounds onions, thinly sliced

4 slices bacon, chopped

3 pounds lean boneless beef chuck, trimmed and cut into 2-inch pieces

½ teaspoon salt

¼ teaspoon ground black pepper

3 tablespoons all-purpose flour

1 can (14½ ounces) beef broth

1 bottle (12 ounces) dark beer (not stout)

½ teaspoon dried thyme

1 bay leaf

1. Preheat oven to 350°F. In 5-quart Dutch oven, heat 2 tablespoons oil over medium-high heat. Add onions and cook until tender and browned, 20 to 25 minutes. Transfer onions to large bowl.

2. In Dutch oven, cook bacon over medium heat until browned; with slotted spoon, transfer to bowl with onions.

3. Pat beef dry with paper towels; sprinkle with salt and pepper. Add half of beef to bacon drippings in Dutch oven and cook over high heat until well browned, using slotted spoon to transfer beef as it is browned to bowl with bacon. Repeat with remaining beef.

4. Reduce heat to medium-high. Add remaining 1 tablespoon oil to Dutch oven. Stir in flour until well blended and cook, stirring constantly, until flour browns. Gradually stir in broth and beer. Cook, stirring constantly, until sauce has thickened and boils.

5. Return beef mixture to Dutch oven; add thyme and bay leaf. Cover and place in oven. Bake until meat is tender, about 2 hours 30 minutes. Skim and discard fat from stew liquid; discard bay leaf.

EACH SERVING About 369 calories | 29 g protein | 14 g carbohydrate | 22 g total fat (7 g saturated) | 93 mg cholesterol | 574 mg sodium.

Choucroute Garni

For sauerkraut lovers! This homey dish, best made in the cold winter months, hails from the Alsace region in eastern France, where the cuisine reflects the influence of neighboring Germany. Serve it with boiled potatoes, crusty bread, and a pot of good mustard.

PREP 20 minutes **COOK** 50 minutes **MAKES** 6 main-dish servings

4 slices bacon, cut into 1-inch pieces

¼ cup water

1 large onion (12 ounces), thinly sliced

2 McIntosh apples, each peeled, cored, cut into quarters, and thinly sliced

2 bags (16 ounces each) sauerkraut, rinsed and drained

1½ cups fruity white wine, such as Riesling

6 juniper berries, crushed

1 bay leaf

6 smoked pork chops, ½ inch thick (4 ounces each)

1 pound kielbasa (smoked Polish sausage), cut into 1½-inch pieces

1. In nonreactive 5-quart Dutch oven, combine bacon and water; cook over medium-low heat until bacon is lightly crisped, about 4 minutes. Add onion and cook, stirring frequently, until onion is tender and golden, about 7 minutes.

2. Add apples and cook until tender, about 3 minutes. Stir in sauerkraut, wine, juniper berries, and bay leaf and heat to boiling. Reduce heat; cover and simmer 15 minutes.

3. Nestle pork chops and kielbasa into sauerkraut mixture; cover and cook until pork chops and sausage are heated through and sauerkraut is tender, about 20 minutes. Remove bay leaf and serve.

EACH SERVING About 524 calories | **27 g protein** | **19 g carbohydrate** | **37 g total fat (13 g saturated)** | **106 mg cholesterol** | **3,151 mg sodium.**

Lamb Shanks with White Beans and Roasted Endive

This hearty braise of rich lamb will warm and cheer you even in the coldest of winter nights (see photo on page 51).

📖 **PREP** 1½ hours **BAKE** 2 hours **MAKES** 8 main-dish servings

WHITE BEANS AND LAMB SHANKS

1 package (16 ounces) dry Great Northern beans

8 small lamb shanks (about 1 pound each)

2½ teaspoons salt

1 teaspoon coarsely ground black pepper

2 tablespoons vegetable oil

6 medium garlic cloves, crushed with side of chef's knife

4 carrots, each peeled and cut into 1-inch pieces

1 large onion, coarsely chopped

¼ cup all-purpose flour

2 tablespoons tomato paste

2 cups dry white wine

1 can (14 to 14½ ounces) chicken broth (1¾ cups)

1 cup water

2 sprigs fresh rosemary, plus 8 sprigs for garnish

ROASTED ENDIVE

1 tablespoon olive oil

½ teaspoon salt

¼ teaspoon coarsely ground black pepper

8 medium heads Belgian endive (about 1½ pounds)

1. Prepare White Beans: In 4-quart saucepan, place beans and enough water to cover by 2 inches; heat to boiling over high heat. Remove saucepan from heat; set aside 40 minutes to soften beans. Drain. (Or, if you prefer, soak beans overnight in cold water. Drain.)

2. Meanwhile, prepare Lamb Shanks: Pat shanks dry with paper towels; sprinkle with 1 teaspoon salt and ½ teaspoon pepper. In 8-quart Dutch oven, heat oil over medium-high heat until very hot but not smoking. Add shanks, in batches, and cook 12 to 15 minutes, turning to brown all sides. Transfer shanks to large bowl as they brown. If necessary, reduce heat to medium before adding second batch of shanks to prevent overbrowning.

3. Preheat oven to 375°F. Add garlic, carrots, and onion to Dutch oven; cook 10 minutes or until browned and tender, stirring frequently. Add flour, tomato paste, and remaining 1½ teaspoons salt and ½ teaspoon pepper. Cook 2 minutes, stirring constantly. Add wine and heat to boiling, stirring until browned bits are loosened from bottom of Dutch oven; boil 5 minutes. Add broth and water; heat to boiling. Stir in beans and 2 sprigs rosemary and return shanks to Dutch oven; heat to boiling. Cover Dutch oven and bake 1 hour.

4. Meanwhile, prepare Roasted Endive: In large bowl, with fork, mix olive oil, salt, and pepper. Trim root ends of endive and cut each lengthwise in half. Toss endive with oil mixture to coat. In 15½" by 10½" jelly-roll pan, arrange endive, cut sides down.

5. After 1 hour, turn shanks over; replace cover. Place endive and shanks in same oven. Bake shanks and endive 1 hour or until meat is fork-tender and easily separates from bone and endive is very tender and bottoms begin to brown.

6. When shanks are done, transfer to large bowl. Skim and discard fat from liquid. Remove and discard rosemary. To serve, onto each of 8 large dinner plates, spoon some beans and cooking liquid; top with a lamb shank and 2 endive halves. Garnish with a rosemary sprig.

EACH SERVING LAMB AND BEANS About 725 calories | 67 g protein | 46 g carbohydrate | 28 g total fat (11 g saturated) / 198 mg cholesterol | 1,110 mg sodium.

EACH SERVING ENDIVE About 30 calories | 1 g protein | 3 g carbohydrate | 2 g total fat (0 g saturated) | 0 mg cholesterol | 145 mg sodium.

Polenta and Sausage Casserole

Layers of creamy polenta, two cheeses, and a sausage-tomato sauce makes this a terrific casserole for a potluck party, buffet, or brunch. The tomato-sausage sauce is also terrific on its own, served over pasta.

PREP I hour **BAKE** 35 minutes **MAKES** 8 main-dish servings

8 ounces sweet Italian-sausage links, casings removed

8 ounces hot Italian-sausage links, casings removed

I tablespoon olive oil

I large onion (12 ounces), chopped

I large stalk celery, chopped

I carrot, peeled and chopped

I can (28 ounces) plum tomatoes in puree

2 cups yellow cornmeal

I can (14½ ounces) chicken broth or 1¾ cups Chicken Broth (page 9)

¾ teaspoon salt

4½ cups boiling water

½ cup freshly grated Parmesan cheese

8 ounces Fontina or mozzarella cheese, shredded (2 cups)

1. Prepare tomato-sausage sauce: In nonreactive 5-quart Dutch oven, cook sweet and hot sausage meat over medium-high heat, breaking up meat with side of spoon, until browned. With slotted spoon, transfer meat to bowl. Discard fat from Dutch oven.

2. Add oil to Dutch oven. Add onion, celery, and carrot and cook over medium-high heat until browned. Stir in sausage and tomatoes with their puree, breaking up tomatoes with side of spoon. Heat to boiling over high heat. Reduce heat; cover Dutch oven and simmer 10 minutes. Remove cover and simmer 10 minutes longer.

3. Preheat oven to 350°F. Prepare polenta: In 4-quart saucepan with wire whisk, mix cornmeal, broth, and salt. Over medium-high heat, add boiling water and cook, whisking constantly, until mixture has thickened, about 5 minutes. Whisk in Parmesan.

4. Grease 13" by 9" baking dish. Evenly spread half of polenta mixture in baking dish; top with half of tomato-sausage sauce, then half of Fontina. Repeat with remaining polenta mixture and sauce.

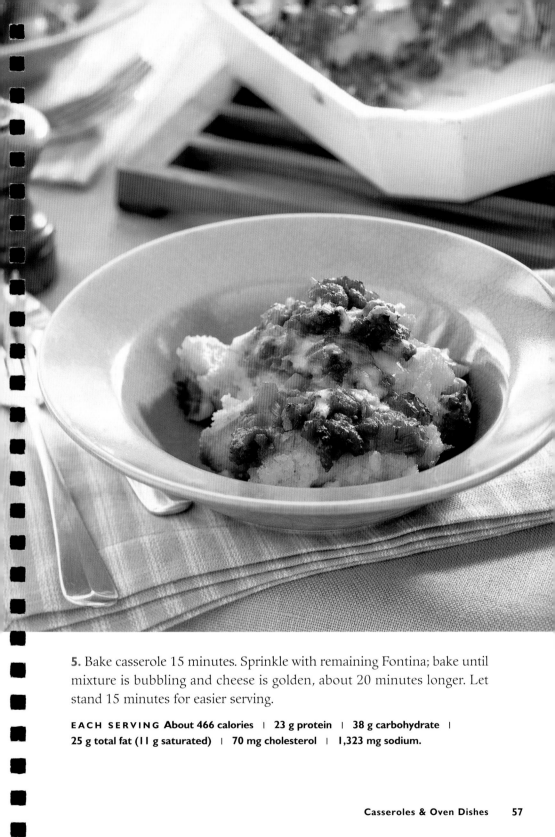

5. Bake casserole 15 minutes. Sprinkle with remaining Fontina; bake until mixture is bubbling and cheese is golden, about 20 minutes longer. Let stand 15 minutes for easier serving.

EACH SERVING About 466 calories | 23 g protein | 38 g carbohydrate | 25 g total fat (11 g saturated) | 70 mg cholesterol | 1,323 mg sodium.

Indian Chicken and Rice Casserole

This dish is usually made with lamb; our lighter recipe calls for skinless chicken breasts.

PREP 30 minutes **BAKE** 35 minutes **MAKES** 6 servings

1 can (14½ ounces) chicken broth or 1¾ cups Chicken Broth (page 9)

1 cup basmati rice

3 garlic cloves, peeled

1 piece (1" by ½") fresh ginger, peeled and coarsely chopped

¼ cup sweetened flaked coconut

1 large onion, halved and thinly sliced

3 teaspoons vegetable oil

1 small red pepper, cut into ½-inch pieces

1 pound skinless, boneless chicken-breast halves, cut into ½-inch pieces

¾ teaspoon ground cumin

¾ teaspoon ground coriander

½ teaspoon salt

⅛ teaspoon ground red pepper (cayenne)

2 cups cauliflower flowerets (about ½ medium head), cut into ½-inch pieces

1 package (10 ounces) frozen peas and carrots

1 can (14½ ounces) diced tomatoes

1 container (8 ounces) plain nonfat yogurt

Raisins, toasted sliced almonds, and toasted sweetened flaked coconut for garnish (optional)

1. Preheat oven to 350°F. In 2-cup measuring cup, add *enough water* to chicken broth to equal 2 cups liquid. In 2-quart saucepan, heat chicken-broth mixture to boiling over high heat. Place rice in shallow 2½-quart casserole; stir in boiling broth mixture. Cover casserole tightly and bake 20 minutes or until rice is tender and all liquid is absorbed. Remove casserole from oven; set aside.

2. Meanwhile, in food processor, with knife blade attached, or in blender, at medium speed, blend garlic, ginger, coconut, and half of onion slices until a paste forms; set aside.

3. In nonstick 12-inch skillet, heat 2 teaspoons vegetable oil over medium heat. Add red pepper and remaining onion slices, and cook until golden, about 10 minutes. With slotted spoon, transfer vegetables to a bowl.

4. Add garlic mixture to same skillet and cook 8 to 10 minutes or until golden. Add chicken pieces and remaining 1 teaspoon oil and cook, stirring occasionally, until chicken is lightly browned on the outside and loses its pink color on the inside. Add cumin, coriander, salt, and ground red pepper and cook 2 minutes longer. Transfer chicken mixture to bowl with vegetables.

5. To same skillet, add cauliflower and ¾ *cup water*; heat to boiling over high heat. Reduce heat to low; cover and simmer 6 minutes. Add frozen peas and carrots, and tomatoes with their juice; heat to boiling over high heat. Reduce heat to low; uncover and cook 2 minutes longer or until cauliflower is tender and peas and carrots are heated through. Transfer cauliflower mixture to bowl with chicken. Stir in yogurt until well mixed.

6. With fork, fluff rice. Top cooked rice with chicken mixture. Bake, uncovered, 15 minutes longer or until heated through. Serve garnished with raisins, toasted almonds, and toasted coconut if you like.

EACH SERVING WITHOUT GARNISHES About 335 calories | 28 g protein | 45 g carbohydrate | 6 g total fat (2 g saturated) | 45 mg cholesterol | 760 mg sodium.

Chicken Shepherd's Pie

Shepherd's pie was originally created as a way to utilize Sunday's leftovers. We've lightened the filling and topped it off with a mantle of creamy, chive-flecked mashed potatoes.

PREP 45 minutes   **BAKE** 20 minutes   **MAKES** 6 main-dish servings

2 pounds all-purpose potatoes (6 medium), peeled and cut into 1-inch pieces

2 tablespoons vegetable oil

2 carrots, peeled and finely chopped

1 large onion (12 ounces), finely chopped

1 large red pepper, finely chopped

2 tablespoons butter or margarine

1 teaspoon salt

¾ cup milk

2 tablespoons chopped fresh chives or green onion tops

10 ounces mushrooms, trimmed and thickly sliced

1¼ cups chicken broth

1 tablespoon all-purpose flour

1½ pounds ground chicken meat

¼ teaspoon coarsely ground black pepper

¼ teaspoon dried thyme

2 tablespoons ketchup

1 tablespoon Worcestershire sauce

1. In 3-quart saucepan, combine potatoes and *enough water to cover*; heat to boiling over high heat. Reduce heat; cover and simmer until potatoes are tender, about 15 minutes.

2. Meanwhile, in 12-inch skillet, heat 1 tablespoon oil over medium-high heat. Add carrots and cook 5 minutes. Add onion and red pepper and cook, stirring occasionally, until vegetables are tender and lightly browned, about 10 minutes longer. With slotted spoon, transfer vegetables to bowl.

3. When potatoes are tender, drain. Mash potatoes in saucepan with butter and ½ teaspoon salt. Gradually add milk; mash until mixture is smooth and well blended. Stir in chives; set aside.

4. In same skillet, heat remaining 1 tablespoon oil over medium-high heat. Add mushrooms and cook until well browned, about 10 minutes. Transfer to bowl with vegetables.

5. In 2-cup measuring cup, blend broth and flour until smooth; set aside.

6. Preheat oven to 400°F. In same skillet, cook ground chicken, black pepper, thyme, and remaining ½ teaspoon salt over high heat, stirring occasionally, until chicken is lightly browned and any liquid in skillet has evaporated, 7 to 10 minutes. Stir in ketchup, Worcestershire, cooked vegetables, and broth mixture. Cook, stirring constantly, until liquid has thickened and boils, 3 to 5 minutes.

7. Spoon mixture into a shallow 2-quart casserole; top with mashed potatoes. Place casserole on foil-lined cookie sheet to catch any overflow during baking. Bake until the potato topping is lightly browned, for 20 to 25 minutes.

EACH SERVING About 415 calories | 26 g protein | 33 g carbohydrate | 20 g total fat (6 g saturated) | 109 mg cholesterol | 848 mg sodium.

Country Captain Casserole

Though the exact origin of this well-known dish is often debated, its great flavor is never in dispute. Try it with basmati rice.

PREP 30 minutes **BAKE** I hour **MAKES** 8 main-dish servings

2 tablespoons plus I teaspoon vegetable oil

2 chickens (3½ pounds each), each cut into 8 pieces and skin removed from all but wings

2 medium onions, chopped

I large Granny Smith apple, peeled, cored, and chopped

I large green pepper, chopped

3 large garlic cloves, finely chopped

I tablespoon grated, peeled fresh ginger

3 tablespoons curry powder

½ teaspoon coarsely ground black pepper

¼ teaspoon ground cumin

I can (28 ounces) plum tomatoes in puree

I can (14½ ounces) chicken broth or 1¾ cups Chicken Broth (page 9)

½ cup dark seedless raisins

I teaspoon salt

¼ cup chopped fresh parsley

I. In nonreactive 8-quart Dutch oven, heat 2 tablespoons oil over medium-high heat until very hot. Add chicken, in batches, and cook until golden brown, about 5 minutes per side. With slotted spoon, transfer chicken pieces to bowl as they are browned.

2. Preheat oven to 350°F. In same Dutch oven, heat remaining 1 teaspoon oil over medium-high heat. Add onions, apple, green pepper, garlic, and ginger; cook, stirring frequently, 2 minutes. Reduce heat to medium; cover and cook 5 minutes longer.

3. Stir in curry powder, black pepper, and cumin; cook 1 minute. Add tomatoes with their puree, broth, raisins, salt, and chicken pieces. Heat to boiling over high heat; boil 1 minute. Cover and place in oven. Bake 1 hour. Sprinkle with parsley.

EACH SERVING About 347 calories | 43 g protein | 19 g carbohydrate | 11 g total fat (2 g saturated) | 133 mg cholesterol | 825 mg sodium.

Mustard-Dill Salmon with Herbed Potatoes

This elegant dish is surprisingly simple to make. While the potatoes cook, you can broil the salmon and whip up the no-cook sauce. For a colorful and healthy side dish, sauté snow peas in a nonstick skillet with a teaspoon of vegetable oil.

PREP 20 minutes   **BROIL** 10 minutes   **MAKES** 4 main-dish servings

12 ounces small red potatoes, cut into 1-inch chunks

12 ounces small white potatoes, cut into 1-inch chunks

1½ teaspoons salt

3 tablespoons chopped fresh dill

½ teaspoon coarsely ground black pepper

4 pieces salmon fillet (about 6 ounces each)

2 tablespoons light mayonnaise

1 tablespoon white wine vinegar

2 teaspoons Dijon mustard

¾ teaspoon sugar

1. In 3-quart saucepan, place the potatoes, 1 teaspoon salt, and *enough water to cover*; heat to boiling over high heat. Reduce heat to low; cover and simmer 15 minutes or until potatoes are fork-tender. Drain potatoes and toss with 1 tablespoon dill, ¼ teaspoon salt, and ¼ teaspoon coarsely ground black pepper; keep potatoes warm.

2. Meanwhile, preheat broiler. Grease rack in broiling pan. Place salmon on rack; sprinkle with ⅛ teaspoon of the salt and ⅛ teaspoon coarsely ground black pepper. Broil salmon at closest position to source of heat 8 to 10 minutes, until fish flakes easily.

3. While salmon is broiling, prepare sauce: In small bowl, mix mayonnaise, vinegar, mustard, sugar, remaining 2 tablespoons dill, ⅛ teaspoon salt, and ⅛ teaspoon pepper.

4. Serve salmon with sauce and potatoes.

EACH SERVING About 335 calories | **37 g protein** | **31 g carbohydrate** | **7 g total fat (1 g saturated)** | **86 mg cholesterol** | **655 mg sodium.**

Shrimp Creole

A New Orleans classic, Shrimp Creole makes a good company as well as a family dish. Serve it with corn bread on the side.

PREP 45 minutes   **BAKE** 30 minutes   **MAKES** 6 main-dish servings

1 tablespoon olive oil

1 large onion, diced

1 medium green pepper, coarsely chopped

1 medium red pepper, coarsely chopped

8 ounces ready-to-eat chorizo sausage or pepperoni, cut into ¼-inch-thick slices

2 garlic cloves, minced

1½ cups parboiled rice

1 can (14½ ounces) stewed tomatoes

1 bottle (8 ounces) clam juice

1¼ cups water

1 package (10 ounces) frozen whole okra, thawed

1 pound medium shrimp, shelled and deveined (page 13)

1. Preheat oven to 350°F. In 3- to 3½-quart Dutch oven, heat oil over medium heat until hot. Add onion and peppers and cook 10 minutes or until tender and lightly browned. Add chorizo and garlic and cook 5 minutes longer or until chorizo is lightly browned.

2. Stir in rice, stewed tomatoes, clam juice, and water; heat to boiling over high heat. Cover Dutch oven, place in oven, and bake 20 minutes. Stir okra and shrimp into rice mixture; cover and bake 10 minutes longer or until rice and shrimp are tender.

EACH SERVING About 405 calories | 26 g protein | 34 g carbohydrate | 18 g total fat (6 g saturated) | 127 mg cholesterol | 800 mg sodium.

GH Test Kitchen Tip

Parboiled rice, sometimes called "converted" rice, is put through a steam-pressure process that results in fluffy, separate grains.

Veggie Enchiladas

Fresh cilantro gives this hearty casserole real southwestern flavor.

PREP 25 minutes   BAKE 20 minutes   MAKES 6 main-dish servings

2 teaspoons olive oil

1 small zucchini (8 ounces), cut into ½-inch pieces

1 medium onion, chopped

1 medium red pepper, chopped

2 cans (15 to 19 ounces each) no-salt-added white kidney beans (cannellini), rinsed and drained

½ cup vegetable broth or chicken broth

2 garlic cloves, minced

1 can (15¼ ounces) no-salt-added whole-kernel corn, drained

2 pickled jalapeño chiles, minced, with seeds

1 cup loosely packed fresh cilantro leaves and stems, chopped

6 flour tortillas (8-inch diameter)

1 jar (15½ ounces) mild salsa

⅓ cup shredded Monterey Jack cheese

lime wedges for garnish

1. In nonstick 12-inch skillet, heat olive oil over medium heat. Add zucchini, onion, and red pepper and cook until the vegetables are tender and golden, about 10 to 15 minutes, stirring frequently.

2. Meanwhile, in food processor with knife blade attached or in blender at medium speed, blend half of white kidney beans with broth until almost smooth. Transfer bean mixture to large bowl; stir in remaining beans and set aside.

3. To vegetables in skillet, add garlic and cook 1 minute longer. Stir in corn and jalapeños; cook 2 minutes longer. Transfer vegetable mixture to bowl with beans; stir in cilantro until mixed.

4. Preheat oven to 375°F. Spoon about ¾ cup bean mixture along center of each tortilla. Fold sides of tortilla over filling, overlapping them slightly.

5. Spoon ½ cup salsa into bottom of 13" by 9" glass or ceramic baking dish. Place enchiladas, seam side down, on top of salsa. Spoon remaining salsa over enchiladas; sprinkle with cheese. Bake 20 minutes. Serve with lime wedges.

EACH SERVING About 415 calories | 17 g protein | 70 g carbohydrate | 8 g total fat (2 g saturated) | 6 mg cholesterol | 700 mg sodium.

Spinach and Feta Bread Pudding

If you love the comfort of warm, sweet bread pudding for dessert, treat yourself to this savory version for brunch or supper.

🕐 **PREP** 15 minutes **BAKE** 25 minutes **MAKES** 6 main-dish servings

2 tablespoons margarine or butter

1 medium onion, chopped

6 large eggs

2 cups low-fat (1%) milk

3 tablespoons chopped fresh dill

½ teaspoon freshly grated lemon peel

½ teaspoon salt

½ teaspoon coarsely ground black pepper

1 package (10 ounces) frozen chopped spinach, thawed and squeezed dry

4 ounces feta cheese, cut into ½-inch cubes

8 slices firm white bread, cut into ¾-inch pieces

1. Preheat oven to 350°F. In nonstick 12-inch skillet with oven-safe handle (or cover handle with heavy-duty foil for baking in oven later), melt margarine over medium heat. Add onion and cook until tender, about 10 minutes.

2. In medium bowl, with wire whisk or fork, beat eggs, milk, dill, lemon peel, salt, and pepper until blended. With rubber spatula, stir in onion, spinach, and cheese. Gently stir in bread pieces. Pour mixture into skillet; let stand 15 minutes to allow bread to absorb liquid.

3. Cook mixture over medium-high heat 3 minutes, without stirring, or until mixture begins to set around edge. Place skillet in oven; bake 20 to 25 minutes, until knife inserted in center of bread pudding comes out clean.

4. Remove bread pudding from oven; let stand 5 minutes before serving. To serve, cut into wedges.

EACH SERVING About 295 calories | 16 g protein | 25 g carbohydrate | 15 g total fat (6 g saturated) | 233 mg cholestero | 655 mg sodium.

Stuffed Baby Eggplants

These "boats" capture the flavors of sunny Greece, with feta, olives, and mint.

⊘ **PREP** 30 minutes **COOK** 35 minutes **MAKES** 6 main-dish servings

6 small Italian eggplants
  (8 ounces each)

3 tablespoons olive oil

1 cup long-grain white rice

1¼ teaspoons salt

1 medium red onion,
  coarsely chopped

1 medium red pepper, cut into
  ¼-inch dice

1 garlic clove, minced

½ teaspoon dried mint

¼ teaspoon coarsely ground
  black pepper

1 tablespoon fresh lemon juice

2 ounces feta cheese, crumbled
  (½ cup)

6 large pitted green olives,
  coarsely chopped

lemon wedges

1. Preheat oven to 450°F. Cut each eggplant lengthwise in half. Rub cut sides of eggplants with 2 tablespoons olive oil. Place eggplants, cut side down, in 15½" by 10½" jelly-roll pan and bake 20 to 25 minutes until tender. Remove jelly-roll pan with eggplants from oven. Turn oven control to 400°F.

2. While eggplants are baking, in 2-quart saucepan, heat rice, ½ teaspoon salt, and *2 cups water* to boiling over high heat. Reduce heat to low; cover and simmer 15 to 18 minutes, until rice is tender and liquid is absorbed.

3. With spoon, gently scoop out most of the flesh from each eggplant half, leaving about ¼-inch-thick shell. Coarsely chop eggplant flesh and spoon into bowl. Sprinkle eggplant shells with ¼ teaspoon salt. Set eggplant flesh and shells aside.

4. In nonstick 12-inch skillet, heat remaining 1 tablespoon olive oil over medium heat until hot. Add onion and red pepper and cook until vegetables are tender, about 10 minutes, stirring frequently. Add garlic, mint, black pepper, and remaining ½ teaspoon salt; cook 1 minute longer. Stir in eggplant flesh and cook 5 to 10 minutes, stirring often. Stir in lemon juice.

5. Spoon rice into eggplant shells; top with eggplant mixture. Return to same jelly-roll pan. Sprinkle feta cheese and chopped olives over filled eggplants. Bake 10 minutes or until heated through. Serve with lemon wedges.

EACH SERVING About 275 calories | 6 g protein | 42 g carbohydrate | 10 g total fat (3 g saturated) | 8 mg cholesterol | 575 mg sodium.

Curried Sweet Potatoes and Lentils

This hearty vegetarian entrée tastes even better with a dollop of plain yogurt and a squeeze of fresh lime juice. Serve with a green salad.

PREP 15 minutes   **COOK** 30 minutes   **MAKES** 4 main-dish servings

1 tablespoon olive oil

1 medium onion, chopped

2 garlic cloves, minced

1 tablespoon curry powder

3 medium sweet potatoes
   (1½ pounds), peeled and cut
   into 1-inch chunks

1 cup lentils, rinsed and picked over

½ cup long-grain white rice

½ teaspoon salt

1 can (14½ ounces) vegetable broth
   or chicken broth

¼ cup loosely packed fresh
   cilantro leaves

1. In nonstick 12-inch skillet, heat olive oil over medium heat until hot. Add onion and cook 5 minutes, stirring often. Add garlic and curry powder, and cook 1 minute longer, stirring constantly.

2. Stir in sweet potatoes, lentils, rice, salt, broth, and *2½ cups water*; heat to boiling over medium-high heat. Reduce heat to low; cover and simmer 30 minutes or until lentils and rice are tender and almost all liquid is absorbed. Let stand 5 minutes. Sprinkle with cilantro to serve.

EACH SERVING About 460 calories | 16 g protein | 87 g carbohydrate |
5 g total fat (1 g saturated) | 0 mg cholesterol | 630 mg sodium.

Cabbage and Bulgur Casserole

We layered Napa cabbage with a filling that is healthy and tastes good too. Nutty-tasting bulgur is an especially easy grain to cook with because it doesn't need to be watched or stirred—you simply let it absorb boiling water until tender.

PREP 45 minutes   **BAKE** 40 minutes   **MAKES** 6 main-dish servings

1½ cups bulgur (cracked wheat)

1 tablespoon vegetable oil

2 medium carrots, peeled and diced

2 medium stalks celery, diced

1 medium red pepper, diced

½ small head **Napa (Chinese) cabbage** (about 1¾ pounds), cut crosswise into 2-inch pieces to equal about 12 cups leafy tops and 2 cups crunchy stems

3 garlic cloves, crushed with garlic press

3 green onions, sliced

2 tablespoons minced, peeled fresh ginger

2 tablespoons plus 1 teaspoon soy sauce

2 tablespoons seasoned rice vinegar

1 can (14½ ounces) diced tomatoes

2 tablespoons brown sugar

2 tablespoons chopped fresh parsley

1. Preheat the oven to 350°F. In a 2-quart saucepan, heat *1½ cups water* to boiling over high heat; stir in bulgur. Remove saucepan from heat; cover and set aside.

2. In 5-quart Dutch oven, heat vegetable oil over medium-high heat. Add carrots, celery, and red pepper; cook 5 minutes. Add cabbage stems and cook 7 minutes longer or until vegetables are tender.

3. Reduce heat to low; add garlic, green onions, and ginger and cook 1 minute longer, stirring. Add *½ cup water*; heat to boiling over high heat. Reduce heat to low; simmer 1 minute, stirring. Remove Dutch oven from heat; stir in 2 tablespoons of the soy sauce, 1 tablespoon rice vinegar, and cooked bulgur.

4. In small bowl, combine the tomatoes with their juice, brown sugar, the remaining 1 tablespoon rice vinegar, and 1 teaspoon soy sauce.

5. In 3-quart casserole, place half of cabbage leaves; top with the bulgur mixture, then remaining cabbage leaves. Spoon tomato mixture over top. Cover casserole and bake 40 minutes or until hot in the center and top layer of cabbage leaves is wilted. Sprinkle with chopped parsley before serving.

EACH SERVING About 220 calories | 7 g protein | 43 g carbohydrate | 3 g total fat (0 g saturated) | 0 mg cholesterol | 800 mg sodium

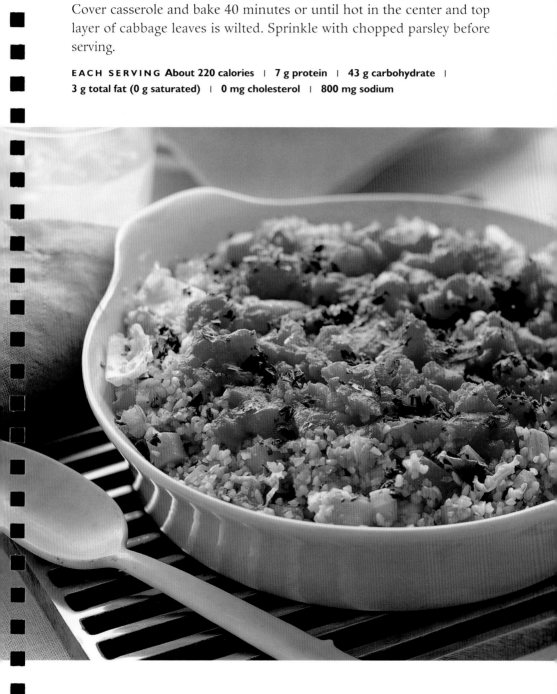

Spaghetti Pie with Prosciutto and Peas

For a healthy twist, try making this with whole wheat spaghetti.

PREP 25 minutes **BAKE** 15 minutes **MAKES** 6 main-dish servings

8 ounces thick spaghetti

4 large eggs

2 large egg whites

1 container (15 ounces) part-skim ricotta cheese

¾ cup reduced-fat (2%) milk

⅛ teaspoon ground nutmeg

¼ teaspoon salt

¼ teaspoon ground black pepper

1 tablespoon margarine or butter

1 bunch green onions, cut into ¼-inch pieces (about 1 cup)

1 cup frozen peas

6 thin slices prosciutto (about 3 ounces)

1. Preheat oven to 350°F. In large saucepot, cook spaghetti 2 minutes less than label directs.

2. Meanwhile, in medium bowl, whisk eggs, egg whites, ricotta, milk, nutmeg, salt, and pepper until blended. Set aside. In oven-safe nonstick 12-inch skillet, melt margarine over medium heat. Add green onions and cook about 5 minutes or until softened. Remove skillet from heat.

3. Drain spaghetti. To green onions in skillet, add spaghetti and frozen peas; toss to combine. Pour egg mixture over pasta and arrange prosciutto slices on top.

4. Place skillet over medium-high heat and cook 3 to 5 minutes or until edges just begin to set. Place skillet in oven and bake 15 minutes or until center is set. Slide pie onto large plate to serve.

EACH SERVING About 375 calories | 25 g protein | 38 g carbohydrate | 13 g total fat (6 g saturated) | 175 mg cholesterol | 700 mg sodium.

Stir-Fries &
Skillet Suppers

**Butternut-Squash
Risotto with Sage
recipe on page 104**

Spicy Tangerine Beef

Sweet, juicy tangerines are the perfect complement to beef and broccoli. Sliced pork tenderloin can be substituted for the beef, if you prefer. Serve over rice.

⏱ **PREP** 25 minutes **COOK** 25 minutes **MAKES** 4 main-dish servings

4 tangerines or 3 medium navel oranges

3 tablespoons vegetable oil

I boneless beef top sirloin steak (12 ounces), thinly sliced crosswise

2 tablespoons plus ½ teaspoon cornstarch

I large bunch broccoli (1½ pounds), cut into flowerets, stems peeled and cut into ¼-inch-thick slices

3 medium green onions, cut diagonally into 2-inch pieces

I medium red pepper, thinly sliced

3 garlic cloves, minced

I tablespoon minced, peeled fresh ginger

3 tablespoons soy sauce

¼ teaspoon crushed red pepper

1. Cut peel and white pith from 1 tangerine or orange. Over small bowl, cut on either side of membranes to remove each segment, allowing fruit and juice to drop into bowl; set aside. From remaining fruit, with vegetable peeler, remove eight 3-inch-long strips peel (about ¾ inch wide each). With knife, remove any pith from peel. Squeeze ¾ cup juice.

2. In 12-inch skillet, heat 2 tablespoons vegetable oil over high heat until hot. Add strips of peel and cook until lightly browned, about 3 minutes. Remove peel to large bowl.

3. Meanwhile, on waxed paper, toss beef slices with 2 tablespoons cornstarch to coat evenly. Cook half of beef until crisp and lightly browned on both sides, about 5 minutes; remove to bowl with peel. Repeat with remaining 1 tablespoon vegetable oil and beef.

4. Add broccoli and *2 tablespoons water* to skillet. Reduce heat to medium; cover and cook 2 minutes. Increase heat to high. Remove cover and add green onions and red pepper; cook 2 minutes, stirring. Add garlic and ginger; cook 1 minute longer.

5. Meanwhile, in cup, stir juice, soy sauce, crushed red pepper, and the remaining ½ teaspoon cornstarch until blended.

6. Add juice mixture and cook until sauce thickens slightly and boils, stirring. Return beef mixture to skillet. Add citrus segments with any juice in bowl; gently toss to combine.

EACH SERVING About 335 calories ∣ 22 g protein ∣ 24 g carbohydrate ∣ 19 g total fat (4 g saturated) ∣ 42 mg cholesterol ∣ 860 mg sodium.

Beef Stir-Fry with Arugula

For a speedy weeknight meal, there's nothing like a stir-fry. To round out the menu, serve this one over rice or couscous with chilled red grapes for dessert.

PREP 10 minutes **COOK** 10 minutes **MAKES** 4 main-dish servings

4 teaspoons vegetable oil

1 bunch green onions, cut into 1½-inch pieces

1 package (8 ounces) sliced mushrooms

1 package (16 ounces) sliced beef for stir-fry (see Tip)

3 tablespoons soy sauce

3 tablespoons balsamic vinegar

2 tablespoons brown sugar

2 bunches arugula or 2 packages (8 ounces each) prewashed spinach

1. In nonstick 12-inch skillet, heat 2 teaspoons oil over medium-high heat. Add green onions and mushrooms and cook until tender and brown, about 5 minutes, stirring often. Remove to bowl.

2. In same skillet, heat 1 teaspoon oil. Add half the beef and cook, stirring constantly, until beef just loses its pink color. Remove to bowl with vegetables. Cook remaining beef as above, adding remaining 1 teaspoon oil.

3. In cup, mix soy sauce, balsamic vinegar, and brown sugar. Return beef mixture to skillet; stir in soy-sauce mixture. Cook 1 minute to heat through, stirring. Remove from heat; stir in half the arugula.

4. Spoon the beef mixture over remaining arugula on platter.

EACH SERVING About 260 calories | 29 g protein | 18 g carbohydrate | 15 g total fat (5 g saturated) | 48 mg cholesterol | 875 mg sodium.

GH Test Kitchen Tip

If you can't find precut beef, thinly slice a 1-pound piece of round steak.

Red Flannel Hash

The trick to great hash is to avoid overstirring. Let it cook undisturbed long enough to become crisp and golden. Serve by the plateful with a cucumber-and-dill salad.

PREP 15 minutes   **COOK** 30 minutes   **MAKES** 4 main-dish servings

1 tablespoon butter or margarine

1 tablespoon vegetable oil

1 jumbo onion (about 1 pound), chopped

2 large stalks celery, cut into ½-inch pieces

1 can (14½ ounces) whole beets, drained and cut into ½-inch pieces

4 cups bite-size pieces cooked potatoes (reserved from **Corned Beef with Cabbage and Potatoes,** page 84)

1½ cups bite-size pieces cooked corned beef (reserved from **Corned Beef with Cabbage and Potatoes,** page 84), about 6 ounces

½ teaspoon salt

¼ teaspoon coarsely ground black pepper

1 tablespoon chopped fresh parsley

1. In nonstick 12-inch skillet, heat butter with oil over medium heat. Add onion and celery and cook 15 minutes or until lightly browned and tender, stirring occasionally.

2. Increase heat to medium-high; add beets, potatoes, corned beef, salt, and pepper, and cook 15 minutes or until browned, stirring occasionally. Sprinkle with parsley to serve.

EACH SERVING About 415 calories | 19 g protein | 62 g carbohydrate | 11 g total fat (3 g saturated) | 40 mg cholesterol | 1,065 mg sodium.

Spicy Beef with Couscous

This curry is on the milder side, so it's great for the whole family. The addition of raisins to the couscous lends an unexpected sweetness.

PREP 30 minutes **COOK** 15 minutes **MAKES** 4 main-dish servings

1 tablespoon vegetable oil

1 medium onion, chopped

2 garlic cloves, crushed with garlic press

1 teaspoon minced, peeled fresh ginger

1 pound lean (90%) ground beef

1 tablespoon curry powder

1 teaspoon garam masala spice mix

½ teaspoon salt

1 small yellow summer squash (about 6 ounces), cut into ½-inch chunks

1 cup Chicken Broth (page 9)

1 cup frozen peas

½ cup loosely packed fresh cilantro leaves, chopped

1 cup plain couscous

⅓ cup golden raisins

1. In nonstick 12-inch skillet, heat oil over medium-high heat. Add onion and cook 3 minutes or until golden. Stir in garlic and ginger; cook 1 minute.

2. Stir in ground beef and cook, breaking up meat with side of spoon, about 5 minutes, or until meat is no longer pink. Stir in curry powder, garam masala, and salt; cook 30 seconds. Add squash and cook 2 minutes.

3. Add broth and frozen peas; cook until slightly thickened and flavors blend. Stir in cilantro.

4. Meanwhile, prepare couscous as label directs but add raisins with water.

5. Fluff couscous with fork and serve with beef mixture.

EACH SERVING About 520 calories | 34 g protein | 57 g carbohydrate | 16 g total fat (5 g saturated) | 69 mg cholesterol | 650 mg sodium.

Q: I know what couscous is, but lately I've seen mentions of *Israeli* couscous. What is it?

A: Medium-grain couscous, made from semolina, is what most of us are used to buying—usually imported from France in the past, it's now produced in the United States, too, and is front and center on many supermarket shelves. Israeli couscous (sometimes labeled "toasted couscous") is sold in specialty stores and Middle Eastern groceries. It's coarse, and about 4 times bigger than medium couscous; it's comparable to *acini di pepe*, the tiny pasta. Israeli couscous can be boiled, steamed, or combined with boiling water and covered until the water is absorbed. It's chewier than the regular kind and looks pretty in summer salads and side dishes made with vegetables.

Corned Beef with Cabbage and Potatoes

A horseradish-mustard sauce dresses up an old favorite. Prepare the recipe over the weekend, then use the leftovers to make Red Flannel Hash (page 81) during the week, when time is at a premium.

🕑 **PREP** 30 minutes **COOK** 3 hours 25 minutes **MAKES** 8 main-dish servings

CORNED BEEF AND VEGETABLES

1 corned-beef brisket (about 4½ pounds), trimmed of excess fat

20 whole black peppercorns

5 whole allspice

5 garlic cloves, unpeeled

2 bay leaves

4 pounds all-purpose potatoes, peeled and each cut into quarters

1 pound carrots, peeled

1 pound parsnips, peeled

1 medium head green cabbage (about 3 pounds), cut into 8 wedges, with core attached

HORSERADISH-MUSTARD SAUCE

½ cup Dijon mustard with seeds

2 tablespoons pure maple syrup

1 tablespoon prepared white horseradish

chopped fresh parsley for garnish

1. Prepare Corned Beef and Vegetables: In 8-quart Dutch oven or saucepot, place brisket, peppercorns, allspice, garlic, bay leaves, and enough *water* to cover; heat to boiling over high heat. Reduce heat to low; cover and simmer 2 hours 30 minutes.

2. Add quartered potatoes, whole carrots, and whole parsnips to Dutch oven; heat to boiling over high heat. Reduce heat to low; cover and simmer 30 minutes or until meat and vegetables are tender. With tongs and slotted spoon, transfer meat and vegetables to warm platter; cover and keep warm.

3. Add cabbage to liquid in Dutch oven; heat to boiling over high heat. Reduce heat to low; cover and simmer 5 minutes or until cabbage is tender.

4. Meanwhile, prepare Horseradish-Mustard Sauce: In small bowl, mix mustard, maple syrup, and horseradish until smooth; set sauce aside.

5. Drain cabbage and add to platter with meat. Thinly slice meat and serve with vegetables and Horseradish-Mustard Sauce. Garnish with chopped fresh parsley.

EACH SERVING About 520 calories | 41 g protein | 64 g carbohydrate | 12 g total fat (4 g saturated) | 105 mg cholesterol | 1,450 mg sodium.

Orange Pork and Asparagus Stir-Fry

Asparagus is graded by size: small, standard, large, and jumbo. All are equally tender, but we call for thin asparagus here because it cooks quickly. Serve over rice.

⏱ **PREP** 20 minutes **COOK** 6 minutes **MAKES** 4 main-dish servings

2 navel oranges

1 teaspoon olive oil

1 whole pork tenderloin (about 12 ounces) trimmed, thinly sliced diagonally

¾ teaspoon salt

¼ teaspoon ground black pepper

1½ pounds thin asparagus, trimmed and each stalk cut in half

1 garlic clove, crushed with garlic press

¼ cup water

kumquats on the stem for garnish (optional)

1. From 1 orange, grate 1 teaspoon peel and squeeze ¼ cup juice. Cut off peel and white pith from remaining orange. Cut orange into ¼-inch slices; cut each slice into quarters.

2. In nonstick 12-inch skillet, heat ½ teaspoon oil over medium-high heat until hot but not smoking. Add half the pork and sprinkle with ¼ teaspoon salt and ⅛ teaspoon pepper; cook 2 minutes or until pork just loses its pink color, stirring frequently. Transfer pork to plate. Repeat with remaining ½ teaspoon oil, pork, ¼ teaspoon salt, and remaining ⅛ teaspoon pepper. Transfer pork to same plate.

3. To same skillet, add asparagus, garlic, orange peel, remaining ¼ teaspoon salt, and water; cover and cook about 2 minutes or until asparagus is tender crisp, stirring occasionally. Return pork to skillet. Add orange juice and orange pieces; heat through, stirring often. Garnish with kumquats if you like.

EACH SERVING About 165 calories | 24 g protein | 8 g carbohydrate | 4 g total fat (1 g saturated) | 50 mg cholesterol | 495 mg sodium.

Spicy Peanut Pork

Asian spices and peanut butter turn pork chops into a sensational supper. Try this tasty combination over steamed rice or Asian noodles.

PREP 15 minutes   **COOK** about 15 minutes   **MAKES** 4 main-dish servings

4 boneless pork loin chops, ¾ inch thick (5 ounces each), well trimmed

¼ teaspoon coarsely ground black pepper

½ teaspoon salt

4 medium green onions, cut into 1-inch diagonal slices

8 ounces snow peas, strings removed

1 tablespoon minced, peeled fresh ginger

3 garlic cloves, crushed with garlic press

¼ cup creamy peanut butter

1 tablespoon sugar

1 tablespoon soy sauce

⅛ teaspoon ground red pepper (cayenne)

¾ cup water

1. Pat pork chops dry with paper towels. Sprinkle pork chops with pepper and ¼ teaspoon salt.

2. Heat nonstick 12-inch skillet over medium-high heat until hot. Add pork chops and cook 4 minutes; turn pork over and cook 3 to 4 minutes longer, until lightly browned on the outside and still slightly pink on the inside. Transfer pork to platter; cover with foil to keep warm.

3. To same skillet, add green onions, snow peas, and remaining ¼ teaspoon salt, and cook over medium heat 4 minutes, stirring frequently. Stir in ginger and garlic; cook 1 minute. Return pork to skillet.

4. Meanwhile, in small bowl, stir peanut butter, sugar, soy sauce, ground red pepper, and water until blended.

5. Pour peanut-butter mixture into same skillet; heat to boiling over medium-high heat. Reduce heat to low; simmer 1 minute.

EACH SERVING About 350 calories | 37 g protein | 13 g carbohydrate | 17 g total fat (5 g saturated) | 76 mg cholesterol | 685 mg sodium.

Polenta with Sausage and Peppers

We used ready-to-slice polenta from the refrigerated section of the supermarket, making this dish super-easy to prepare.

PREP 15 minutes **COOK** 25 minutes **MAKES** 4 main-dish servings

12 ounces hot and/or sweet Italian-sausage links, casings removed

1 package (24 ounces) precooked polenta, cut into 16 slices

1 tablespoon olive oil

1 medium onion, thinly sliced

1 medium red pepper, thinly sliced

1 garlic clove, crushed with garlic press

½ cup chicken broth

1. Preheat broiler. Heat nonstick 12-inch skillet over medium-high heat until hot. Add sausage and cook until browned, about 10 minutes, stirring occasionally and breaking up sausage with side of spoon. With slotted spoon, transfer sausage to medium bowl; wipe skillet clean with paper towels.

2. Spray 15½" by 10½" jelly-roll pan with nonstick cooking spray. Place polenta slices in pan; spray to coat. With pan at closest position to source of heat, broil polenta slices 10 minutes, turning slices over halfway through cooking.

3. Meanwhile, in same skillet, heat olive oil over medium-high heat until hot. Add onion and pepper and cook until tender and lightly browned, 8 to 10 minutes, stirring occasionally. Add garlic and sausage; cook 1 minute, stirring. Add chicken broth and heat to boiling. Return mixture to bowl; keep warm.

4. Serve the polenta slices topped with the sausage mixture.

EACH SERVING About 360 calories | 12 g protein | 31 g carbohydrate | 21 g total fat (6 g saturated) | 45 mg cholesterol | 1,150 mg sodium.

Kielbasa and Red Cabbage

It's worth a trip to a Polish butcher for homemade kielbasa to make this stick-to-your-ribs skillet meal. Try serving over mashed potatoes.

PREP 15 minutes **COOK** 40 minutes **MAKES** 4 main-dish servings

2 tablespoons butter or margarine

1 small onion, chopped

1 small head red cabbage
(1½ pounds), thinly sliced

2 Golden Delicious apples, peeled, cored, and thinly sliced

½ cup apple juice

3 tablespoons red wine vinegar

1 tablespoon sugar

1 teaspoon salt

1 pound kielbasa (smoked Polish sausage), cut crosswise into 2-inch pieces

1. In nonstick 10-inch skillet, melt butter over medium heat. Add onion and cook, stirring, until tender. Add cabbage, apples, apple juice, vinegar, sugar, and salt; heat to boiling. Reduce heat to low; cover and simmer for 15 minutes.

2. Add kielbasa to cabbage mixture; heat to boiling over high heat. Reduce heat; cover and simmer 15 minutes.

EACH SERVING About 524 calories | 18 g protein | 32 g carbohydrate | 37 g total fat (15 g saturated) | 92 mg cholesterol | 1,883 mg sodium.

GH Test Kitchen Tip

We used Golden Delicious for this dish, but Gala, Fuji, or Jonagold would also be good.

Spaghetti Squash with Smoked Mozzarella and Chicken

We microwaved the squash to speed up the cooking time. While it cooks, sauté the onion and chicken. Try this over brown rice.

PREP 15 minutes   **MICROWAVE** 12 minutes   **MAKES** 4 main-dish servings

1 medium spaghetti squash
(about 2½ pounds)

1 tablespoon olive oil

1 large onion, thinly sliced

12 ounces chicken breast cut for
stir-fry

½ teaspoon salt

¼ teaspoon coarsely ground
black pepper

2 medium tomatoes, diced

2 ounces smoked mozzarella or
smoked Gouda cheese

¼ cup loosely packed fresh basil
leaves, thinly sliced

1. With tip of sharp knife, pierce squash in about 10 places. Microwave on High 6 to 7 minutes. Turn squash over and pierce in another 10 places; microwave 6 to 7 minutes longer or until squash is soft to the touch.

2. Meanwhile, in nonstick 12-inch skillet, heat olive oil over medium heat. Add onion and cook until tender and golden, about 8 minutes, stirring occasionally.

3. Add chicken, ¼ teaspoon salt, and ⅛ teaspoon pepper and cook until chicken loses its pink color throughout, about 8 minutes, stirring occasionally.

4. When squash is done, cut lengthwise in half; discard seeds. With fork, gently scrape squash lengthwise and lift out pulp in strands as it becomes free; place in large bowl. Discard squash skin.

5. Mix tomatoes, cheese, and remaining ¼ teaspoon salt and ⅛ teaspoon pepper with hot squash. Spoon squash mixture into 4 serving bowls; top with onion and chicken mixture. Sprinkle with basil.

EACH SERVING About 260 calories | 25 g protein | 20 g carbohydrate |
9 g total fat (3 g saturated) | 62 mg cholesterol | 585 mg sodium.

Cashew Chicken Stir-Fry

This stir-fry is a wonderfully quick and balanced meal: lots of protein from the chicken and cashews along with a nice variety of healthy greens.

🕐 **PREP** 25 minutes **COOK** 20 minutes **MAKES** 4 main-dish servings

I cup jasmine rice or long-grain white rice

½ cup **Chicken Broth (page 9)**

¼ cup dry sherry

2 tablespoons soy sauce

I tablespoon cornstarch

I tablespoon grated, peeled fresh ginger

I teaspoon brown sugar

¼ teaspoon salt

2 tablespoons vegetable oil

8 ounces asparagus, trimmed and cut into 2-inch pieces

4 ounces snow peas, strings removed and each cut in half

2 large carrots, peeled and cut into 2" by ⅛" matchstick-thin strips

I bunch green onions, cut into 2-inch pieces

½ cup unsalted cashews

I pound skinless, boneless chicken-breast halves, thinly sliced crosswise

1. Prepare rice as label directs.

2. Meanwhile, in small bowl, whisk broth, sherry, soy sauce, cornstarch, ginger, sugar, and salt; set aside.

3. In nonstick 12-inch skillet, heat 1 tablespoon oil over medium-high heat until hot. Add asparagus and snow peas and cook 4 minutes or until tender-crisp, stirring frequently. Transfer vegetables to large bowl. To same skillet, add carrots, green onions, and cashews; cook 3 minutes, stirring frequently. Transfer to bowl with asparagus.

4. In same skillet, heat remaining 1 tablespoon oil. Add half of chicken and cook 2 to 3 minutes or just until chicken loses its pink color through-out, stirring constantly. With slotted spoon, transfer chicken to bowl with vegetables. Repeat with remaining chicken.

5. Stir broth mixture and add to skillet; heat to boiling, stirring. Boil 1 minute. Return vegetables and chicken to skillet; heat through. Serve with rice.

EACH SERVING About 525 calories | 35 g protein | 58 g carbohydrate | 17 g total fat (3 g saturated) | 66 mg cholesterol | 870 mg sodium.

Q: I have a recipe that calls for trimmed and *peeled* asparagus spears. Do I really have to peel them?

A: No, it isn't necessary, though in many restaurants the stalks are peeled with a vegetable peeler in the same way that carrots are peeled, for a more elegant presentation. Because the darker green outside of the stalk is full of vitamin C, folic acid, and thiamine, however, we prefer to simply trim asparagus. First, check to see if the stalks look tough and woody, although many growers trim them before shipping so the entire stalk is edible. If the end has *not* been trimmed, snap off by holding the base of each stalk firmly and bending it so the end breaks off at the spot where it becomes too tough to eat. Then rinse the asparagus thoroughly to remove any sand or grit. Some people like to remove the little scales along the stalk with a paring knife, but it is not necessary— they're edible too.

Skillet Arroz con Pollo

This dish, popular in Spain and Mexico, literally means "rice with chicken." We've used chicken-breast tenders instead of bone-in pieces to shorten cooking time. A side salad would make for a refreshing contrast.

PREP 15 minutes **COOK** 40 minutes **MAKES** 4 main-dish servings

1 tablespoon olive oil

1 medium onion, finely chopped

1 medium red pepper, cut into 1½-inch pieces

1 cup long-grain white rice

1 garlic clove, minced

⅛ teaspoon ground red pepper (cayenne)

1 strip (3" by ½") fresh lemon peel

¼ teaspoon salt

1 can (14½ ounces) chicken broth

¼ cup dry sherry or water

1 pound chicken-breast tenders, cut into 2-inch pieces

1 cup frozen peas

¼ cup drained salad olives (chopped pimiento-stuffed olives)

½ cup loosely packed fresh cilantro leaves or parsley leaves, chopped

lemon wedges

1. In nonstick 12-inch skillet, heat oil over medium heat until hot. Add onion and red pepper and cook until tender, about 12 minutes, stirring occasionally. Stir in rice, garlic, and ground red pepper; cook 2 minutes. Stir in lemon peel, salt, chicken broth, and sherry; heat to boiling over medium-high heat. Reduce heat to low; cover and simmer for 13 minutes.

2. Stir in chicken tenders; cover and simmer 13 minutes longer or until juices run clear when chicken is pierced with tip of knife and rice is tender, stirring once halfway through cooking time. Stir in frozen peas; cover and heat through. Remove skillet from heat; let stand 5 minutes.

3. To serve, stir in olives and sprinkle with cilantro. Pass lemon wedges to squeeze over each serving.

EACH SERVING About 410 calories | 34 g protein | 49 g carbohydrate | 7 g total fat (2 g saturated) | 66 mg cholesterol | 925 mg sodium.

Peachy Chicken with Basil

Fragrant basil, sweet onion, and juicy fruit slices form the perfect sauce for lean chicken breasts. Spoon over noodles or rice to capture every luscious drop. Serve with a green salad.

🕐 **PREP** 20 minutes   **COOK** 15 minutes   **MAKES** 4 main-dish servings

3 tablespoons all-purpose flour

½ teaspoon salt

½ teaspoon coarsely ground black pepper

4 medium skinless, boneless chicken-breast halves (about 1¼ pounds)

2 tablespoons butter or margarine

¾ cup chicken broth

3 medium peaches (about 1 pound), peeled and sliced

1 small red onion, thinly sliced

¼ teaspoon freshly grated lemon peel

8 large basil leaves, thinly sliced

1. On waxed paper, mix flour, salt, and pepper. Coat the chicken breasts with the seasoned flour.

2. In nonstick 12-inch skillet, melt butter over medium heat. Add chicken and cook 10 to 12 minutes, until juices run clear when thickest part of chicken breast is pierced with tip of knife, turning once. Transfer chicken to platter; keep warm.

3. Add chicken broth to skillet; heat to boiling over high heat. Add peaches, red onion, and lemon peel. Cook, stirring frequently, about 3 minutes or until peaches are softened and sauce is slightly thickened. Stir sliced basil into skillet.

4. Spoon sauce over chicken to serve.

EACH SERVING About 280 calories | 35 g protein | 16 g carbohydrate | 8 g total fat (2 g saturated) | 82 mg cholesterol | 580 mg sodium.

Thai Chicken with Asparagus

A trio of Asian seasonings—ginger, chiles, and Asian fish sauce—turns up the heat in this skillet dinner. If you prefer, use fresh green beans instead of the asparagus. Serve over rice.

PREP 25 minutes **COOK** 30 minutes **MAKES** 4 main-dish servings

1 teaspoon salt

1 pound thin asparagus, trimmed and cut diagonally into 3-inch pieces

1 tablespoon sugar

3 tablespoons Asian fish sauce (see Tip)

2 tablespoons fresh lime juice

1 tablespoon plus 1 teaspoon soy sauce

4 medium skinless, boneless chicken-breast halves (about 1¼ pounds), thinly sliced

3 teaspoons vegetable oil

1 jumbo onion (about 1 pound), thinly sliced

1 piece fresh ginger (about 2" by 1"), peeled and cut into matchstick-thin strips

2 jalapeño chiles, seeded and cut into matchstick-thin strips

2 cups packed fresh basil leaves

1 cup packed fresh cilantro leaves

1. In 10-inch skillet, heat *1 inch water* and salt to boiling over high heat. Add asparagus; heat to boiling. Reduce heat to low; simmer, uncovered, 3 to 5 minutes, until asparagus is just tender-crisp. Drain asparagus; set aside.

2. In medium bowl, mix sugar, fish sauce, lime juice, and soy sauce. Stir in chicken until evenly coated. (Coat chicken just before cooking, because the lime juice will change its texture.)

3. In nonstick 12-inch skillet, heat 2 teaspoons oil over medium-high heat until hot. Add chicken and cook 5 minutes or just until it loses its pink color throughout, stirring occasionally. With tongs or slotted spoon, transfer chicken to a clean bowl, leaving any cooking liquid in skillet.

4. Add onion, ginger, and jalapeños to skillet and cook until onion is tender, about 8 minutes. Transfer onion mixture to bowl with the cooked chicken.

5. In same skillet, heat remaining 1 teaspoon oil over medium heat until hot. Add the asparagus to the skillet and cook until it begins to brown, about 5 minutes, stirring occasionally. Return onion mixture and chicken to skillet; heat through.

6. Toss basil and cilantro leaves with chicken mixture just before serving.

EACH SERVING About 290 calories | **38 g protein** | **21 g carbohydrate** | **6 g total fat (1 g saturated)** | **82 mg cholesterol** | **1,555 mg sodium.**

GH Test Kitchen Tip

Asian fish sauce (*nuoc nam* or *nam pla*) is available in specialty sections of some supermarkets or in Asian groceries.

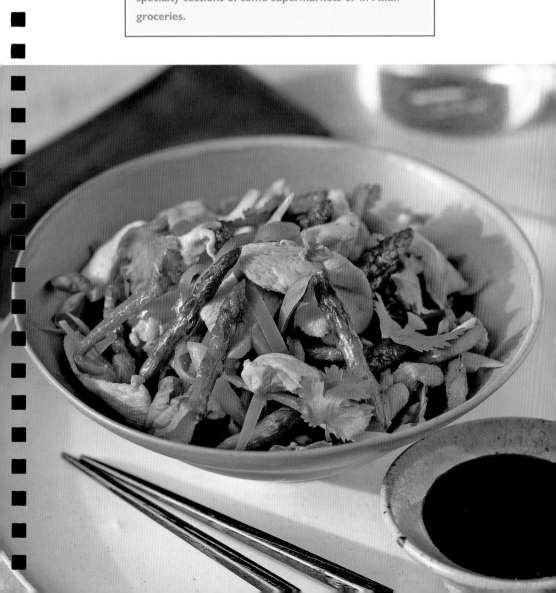

Chicken Breasts with Vegetable Ribbons

Lemon peel, garlic, and parsley add easy elegance and bursts of flavor. An ordinary vegetable peeler is all you need to make the vegetable ribbons. Serve over rice or couscous.

PREP 15 minutes **COOK** 25 minutes **MAKES** 4 main-dish servings

4 medium skinless, boneless chicken-breast halves (about 1¼ pounds)

¼ teaspoon coarsely ground black pepper

½ teaspoon salt

2 garlic cloves, minced

2 teaspoons freshly grated lemon peel

1 tablespoon olive oil

3 medium carrots, peeled

2 medium zucchini (about 8 ounces each)

¾ cup chicken broth

1 cup loosely packed fresh parsley leaves, chopped

1. Sprinkle chicken with pepper and ¼ teaspoon salt. In cup, mix garlic, lemon peel, and remaining ¼ teaspoon salt; set aside.

2. In 12-inch skillet, heat oil over medium-high heat until hot. Add chicken and cook 6 minutes. Reduce heat to medium; turn chicken over and cook 6 to 8 minutes longer, until juices run clear when thickest part of breast is pierced with tip of knife.

3. Meanwhile, with sharp vegetable peeler, peel carrots lengthwise into wide, thin strips. Repeat with zucchini.

4. Transfer chicken to plate; sprinkle with garlic mixture and keep warm. In same skillet, heat broth and *¼ cup water* to boiling over high heat. Reduce heat to medium-low; add carrots and cook, covered, 3 minutes. Add zucchini and cook, covered, 5 to 7 minutes longer, until vegetables are just tender. Stir in all but 1 tablespoon parsley.

5. To serve, spoon vegetable ribbons and broth onto 4 dinner plates; top with chicken. Sprinkle with remaining parsley.

EACH SERVING About 240 calories | 36 g protein | 0 g carbohydrate | 6 g total fat (1 g saturated) | 82 mg cholesterol | 530 mg sodium.

Shrimp Curry and Rice

This tastes as good as classic slow-cooked curry but is ready in a flash.
Serve with crisp flatbreads such as pappadams.

PREP 10 minutes   **COOK** 20 minutes   **MAKES** 4 main-dish servings

1 cup regular long-grain rice

2 teaspoons olive oil

1 medium onion, diced

1 tablespoon curry powder

1 teaspoon mustard seeds

1 pound shelled and deveined fresh or frozen (thawed) large shrimp with tail part of shell left on if you like (page 13)

½ cup light coconut milk (not cream of coconut)

¾ cup frozen peas, thawed

1 cup frozen whole baby carrots, thawed

½ teaspoon salt

chopped fresh cilantro leaves (optional)

1. Prepare rice as label directs but do not add margarine or butter.

2. Meanwhile, in nonstick 12-inch skillet, heat 1 teaspoon olive oil over medium-high heat until hot. Reduce heat to medium; add onion and cook 8 minutes or until tender. Add curry powder and cook 1 minute, stirring. Transfer onion mixture to medium bowl.

3. Increase heat to medium-high. In same skillet, heat remaining 1 teaspoon olive oil until hot. Add mustard seeds; cook 30 seconds, stirring. Add the shrimp and cook 4 minutes or until opaque throughout, stirring frequently.

4. Return onion mixture to skillet; stir in coconut milk, peas, carrots, and salt; heat through. Serve over rice. Sprinkle with cilantro if you like.

EACH SERVING About 390 calories | 30 g protein | 49 g carbohydrate | 8 g total fat (2 g saturated) | 175 mg cholesterol | 490 mg sodium.

Shrimp Risotto with Baby Peas

Be sure to buy shrimp in the shells for this dish. Making a quick stock with the shells gives this pretty risotto a more complex flavor.

PREP 35 minutes **COOK** 55 minutes **MAKES** 4 main-dish servings

4 cups water

1 can (14½ ounces) chicken or vegetable broth or 1¾ cups Chicken Broth (page 9) or Vegetable Broth (page 11)

1 pound medium shrimp, shelled and deveined (page 13), shells reserved

1 tablespoon butter or margarine

1½ teaspoons salt

⅛ teaspoon ground black pepper

1 tablespoon olive oil

1 small onion, finely chopped

2 cups Arborio rice (Italian short-grain rice) or medium-grain rice

½ cup dry white wine

1 cup frozen baby peas

¼ cup chopped fresh parsley

1. In 3-quart saucepan, combine water, broth, and shrimp shells. Heat to boiling over high heat. Reduce heat; simmer 20 minutes. Strain broth through sieve into bowl and measure. If needed, add *water* to equal 5½ cups. Return broth to same clean saucepan; heat to boiling. Reduce heat to maintain simmer; cover.

2. In 4-quart saucepan, melt butter over medium-high heat. Add shrimp, ½ teaspoon salt, and pepper; cook, stirring, just until the shrimp are opaque throughout, about 2 minutes. Transfer to bowl.

3. In same saucepan, heat oil over medium heat. Add onion and cook until tender, about 5 minutes. Add rice and remaining 1 teaspoon salt; cook, stirring frequently, until rice grains are opaque. Add wine; cook until wine has been absorbed. Add about ½ cup simmering broth to rice; stir until liquid has been absorbed. Continue cooking, adding remaining broth ½ cup at a time and stirring after each addition, until all liquid has been absorbed and rice is tender but still firm, about 25 minutes (Risotto should have a creamy consistency.) Stir in frozen peas and shrimp and heat through. Stir in parsley.

EACH SERVING About 511 calories | 28 g protein | 76 g carbohydrate | 10 g total fat (3 g saturated) | 148 mg cholesterol | 1,532 mg sodium.

Chili Scallops with Black-Bean Salsa

A light dusting of spices makes tender sea scallops taste really special. The flavorful salsa can also be served as a side dish with grilled beef or chicken.

PREP 15 minutes **COOK** 3 minutes **MAKES** 4 main-dish servings

1 can (15 to 19 ounces) black beans, rinsed and drained

1 can (15¼ to 16 ounces) whole-kernel corn, drained

¼ cup finely chopped red onion

¼ cup loosely packed fresh cilantro leaves, chopped

2 tablespoons fresh lime juice

½ teaspoon salt

1 pound sea scallops

1 tablespoon chili powder

1 teaspoon sugar

2 teaspoons vegetable oil

cilantro leaves and hot red chiles for garnish

lime wedges (optional)

1. In large bowl, mix black beans, corn, onion, chopped cilantro, lime juice, and ¼ teaspoon salt. Set black-bean salsa aside.

2. Rinse scallops with cold running water to remove sand from crevices; pat dry with paper towels. In medium bowl, mix chili powder, sugar, and remaining ¼ teaspoon salt; add scallops, tossing to coat.

3. In nonstick 12-inch skillet, heat vegetable oil over medium-high heat until very hot. Add scallops and cook 3 to 6 minutes until scallops are lightly browned on the outside and turn opaque throughout, turning once.

4. Arrange black-bean salsa and scallops on 4 dinner plates and garnish with cilantro leaves and red chiles. Serve with lime wedges if you like.

EACH SERVING About 290 calories | 31 g protein | 40 g carbohydrate | 5 g total fat (1 g saturated) | 38 mg cholesterol | 1,005 mg sodium.

Jeweled Cinnamon Couscous

A hearty nonmeat main dish you can whip up in only ten minutes. If you crave something green, toss in a half cup of frozen peas or serve with a crisp salad.

 PREP 5 minutes **COOK** 5 minutes   **MAKES** about 8 cups or 4 main-dish servings

I tablespoon margarine or butter

½ medium red onion, chopped

I package (8 ounces) sliced mushrooms

I can (14 to 14½ ounces) low-sodium vegetable broth

¼ cup water

I can (15 to 19 ounces) low-sodium garbanzo beans

½ cup dried cranberries

½ cup golden raisins

¼ cup dry sherry

I teaspoon salt

½ teaspoon ground cinnamon

¼ teaspoon ground black pepper

I package (10 ounces) plain couscous

1. In deep 12-inch skillet, melt margarine over medium-high heat. Add onion and mushrooms; cook 3 minutes.

2. While mushrooms are cooking, in 1-quart saucepan, heat broth and water to boiling over high heat.

3. Stir beans, cranberries, raisins, sherry, salt, cinnamon, and pepper into mushroom mixture. Remove skillet from heat.

4. Add couscous to skillet; stir in hot broth. Cover and let mixture stand 5 minutes or until liquid is absorbed. Fluff with fork before serving.

EACH SERVING About 570 calories I 19 g protein I 110 g carbohydrate I 6 g total fat (I g saturated) I 0 mg cholesterol I 710 mg sodium.

Butternut-Squash Risotto with Sage

This requires a lot of attention at the range, but it's worth it. If you can, use Arborio rice—it makes the dish extra creamy (see photo on page 77).

PREP 20 minutes **COOK** 50 minutes **MAKES** 4 main-dish servings

1 large butternut squash
(2½ pounds), peeled

1 can (13¾ to 14½ ounces) chicken
or vegetable broth

1 tablespoon butter or margarine

¼ teaspoon coarsely ground
black pepper

3 tablespoons chopped fresh sage

1 teaspoon salt

2 tablespoons olive oil

1 small onion, finely chopped

2 cups Arborio rice (Italian short-
grain rice) or medium-grain rice

⅓ cup dry white wine

½ cup grated Parmesan cheese

1. Cut enough squash into ½-inch chunks to equal 3 cups. Coarsely shred enough remaining squash to equal 2 cups; set aside.

2. In 2-quart saucepan, heat broth and *4 cups water* to boiling over high heat. Reduce heat to low to maintain simmer; cover.

3. In 5-quart Dutch oven or saucepot, melt butter over medium heat. Add squash chunks, pepper, 2 tablespoons chopped sage, and ¼ teaspoon salt. Cook, covered, stirring occasionally, 10 minutes or until squash is tender. Remove squash to small bowl.

4. To same Dutch oven, add oil, shredded squash, onion, and remaining ¾ teaspoon salt and cook, stirring often, until vegetables are tender. Add rice and cook, stirring frequently, 2 minutes. Add wine; cook until absorbed. Add about ½ cup simmering broth to rice, stirring until liquid is absorbed.

5. Continue cooking, adding remaining broth, ½ cup at time, and stirring after each addition until all liquid is absorbed and rice is tender but still firm, about 25 minutes (risotto should have a creamy consistency). Stir in squash chunks, Parmesan, and remaining 1 tablespoon chopped sage and heat through.

EACH SERVING About 700 calories | 17 g protein | 115 g carbohydrate | 4 g total fat (4 g saturated) | 15 mg cholesterol | 1,105 mg sodium.

Fast Fried Rice

The secrets to this dish are quick-cooking brown rice, precut frozen vegetables, and ready-to-use stir-fry sauce.

PREP 5 minutes   **COOK** 10 minutes   **MAKES** 4 main-dish servings

1½ cups quick-cooking brown rice

1 pound firm tofu, drained and cut into 1-inch cubes

6 teaspoons olive oil

1 package (16 ounces) frozen vegetables for stir-fry

2 large eggs, lightly beaten

⅓ cup stir-fry sauce

1. Prepare rice as label directs.

2. Meanwhile, in medium bowl, place 3 layers paper towels. Place tofu on towels and top with 3 more layers paper towels. Gently press the tofu with your hand to extract the excess moisture.

3. In nonstick 12-inch skillet, heat 2 teaspoons oil over medium-high heat until hot. Add frozen vegetables; cover and cook 5 minutes, stirring occasionally. Transfer vegetables to bowl; keep warm.

4. In same skillet, heat remaining 4 teaspoons oil until hot. Add tofu and cook 5 minutes, gently stirring. Stir in rice and cook 4 minutes longer.

5. With spatula, push rice mixture around edge of skillet, leaving space in center. Add eggs to center of skillet; cook 1 minute, stirring eggs until scrambled. Add stir-fry sauce, vegetables, and ¼ *cup water*; cook 1 minute, stirring.

EACH SERVING About 360 calories | 17 g protein | 41 g carbohydrate | 15 g total fat (2 g saturated) | 106 mg cholesterol | 760 mg sodium.

Pastas & Pies

Baked Pasta with
Butternut Squash
recipe on page 132

Beef and Sausage Lasagna

Always let lasagna stand for a good fifteen minutes after baking so the ingredients have time to settle—it makes for easier cutting.

◎ **PREP** I hour **BAKE** 45 minutes **MAKES** 10 main-dish servings

8 ounces hot Italian-sausage links, casings removed

8 ounces ground beef chuck

I medium onion, chopped

I can (28 ounces) plum tomatoes

2 tablespoons tomato paste

I¼ teaspoons salt

12 lasagna noodles (10 ounces)

I container (15 ounces) part-skim ricotta cheese

I large egg

¼ cup chopped fresh parsley

⅛ teaspoon coarsely ground black pepper

8 ounces part-skim mozzarella cheese, shredded (2 cups)

I. Prepare meat sauce: In 4-quart saucepan, cook sausage, ground beef, and onion over high heat, breaking up sausage and meat with side of spoon, until meat is well browned. Discard fat. Add tomatoes with their juice, tomato paste, and 1 teaspoon salt. Heat to boiling, breaking up tomatoes with side of spoon. Reduce heat; cover and simmer, stirring occasionally, 30 minutes.

2. Meanwhile, in large saucepot, cook lasagna noodles as label directs but do not add salt to water. Drain and rinse with cold running water. Return to saucepot with *enough cold water to cover*.

3. Preheat oven to 375°F. In medium bowl, stir ricotta, egg, parsley, remaining ¼ teaspoon salt, and pepper until well combined.

4. Drain noodles on clean kitchen towels. In 13" by 9" baking dish, arrange 6 lasagna noodles, overlapping to fit. Spread with all of ricotta mixture and sprinkle with half of mozzarella; top with half of meat sauce. Cover with remaining 6 noodles and spread with remaining meat sauce. Sprinkle with remaining mozzarella.

5. Cover lasagna with foil and bake 30 minutes. Remove foil and bake until sauce is bubbling and top has lightly browned, about 15 minutes longer. Let stand 15 minutes for easier serving.

EACH SERVING About 363 calories | 23 g protein | 31 g carbohydrate | 16 g total fat (7 g saturated) | 74 mg cholesterol | 780 mg sodium.

Tamale Pie

Enjoy the great taste of tamales with less work. A green salad with grapefruit sections and sliced avocado makes a nice accompaniment.

PREP 25 minutes **BAKE** 45 minutes **MAKES** 6 main-dish servings

2 teaspoons vegetable oil

1 medium onion, chopped

1 pound ground beef chuck

1 tablespoon chili powder

1 teaspoon ground cumin

1 cup medium-hot salsa

1 can (15¼ to 16 ounces) whole-kernel corn, drained

4 cups water

1 cup cornmeal

1 teaspoon salt

2 ounces Cheddar cheese, shredded (½ cup)

1. Preheat oven to 350°F. In nonstick 12-inch skillet, heat oil over medium-high heat; add onion and cook until tender and golden, about 5 minutes. Stir in ground beef and cook, breaking up meat with side of spoon, until meat is browned, about 5 minutes. Skim and discard any fat. Stir in chili powder and cumin and cook 2 minutes longer. Remove from heat and stir in salsa and corn.

2. In 2-quart saucepan, heat water to boiling. With wire whisk, gradually whisk in cornmeal and salt. Cook over medium heat, whisking frequently, 5 minutes.

3. Pour half of cornmeal mixture into shallow 2-quart casserole. Spoon beef mixture over cornmeal; spoon remaining cornmeal over beef and sprinkle Cheddar on top. Bake 45 minutes. Remove casserole from oven and let stand 15 to 25 minutes before serving.

EACH SERVING About 334 calories | 21 g protein | 33 g carbohydrate | 13 g total fat (5 g saturated) | 57 mg cholesterol | 1,026 mg sodium.

GH Test Kitchen Tip

If you prefer firm slices, let the pie rest for at least twenty-five minutes before serving.

Bacon and Cheese Strata

You can assemble this strata a day ahead, then pop it in the oven right from the refrigerator. A side salad will complete the meal.

PREP 20 minutes   **BAKE** 40 minutes   **MAKES** 6 main-dish servings

6 slices bacon

2 tablespoons Dijon mustard with seeds

12 slices firm white bread

6 ounces Gruyère cheese, shredded (1½ cups)

9 large eggs

3 cups whole milk

½ teaspoon salt

¼ teaspoon ground black pepper

1. On microwave-safe plate, place bacon on double thickness of paper towels. Cover with 1 paper towel. Cook on High 2 to 3 minutes or until browned. Let stand 5 minutes or until cool and crisp. Coarsely crumble bacon.

2. Meanwhile, grease 13" by 9" ceramic or glass baking dish.

3. Spread mustard on 1 side of each bread slice. Arrange 6 bread slices, mustard side up, in bottom of baking dish, cutting slices to fit if necessary. Sprinkle with half of cheese. Top with all but 2 tablespoons crumbled bacon, then remaining bread slices, mustard side up.

4. In large bowl, with wire whisk, beat eggs, milk, salt, and pepper until blended. Slowly pour egg mixture over bread slices; press bread down to help it absorb egg mixture. If necessary, spoon egg mixture over any un-coated bread. Top with remaining cheese and bacon. Let stand at room temperature 15 minutes or cover and refrigerate overnight.

5. Preheat oven to 350°F. Bake strata 40 minutes or until puffed and golden and knife inserted in center comes out clean. Let stand at least 10 minutes before serving.

EACH SERVING About 480 calories | 28 g protein | 32 g carbohydrate | 26 g total fat (12 g saturated) | 372 mg cholesterol | 840 mg sodium.

Pepperoni Rigatoni Bake

Serve this simple, hearty dish with a green salad to lighten things up.

PREP 25 minutes   COOK 20 minutes   MAKES 6 main-dish servings

1 package (16 ounces) rigatoni or penne pasta

2 large eggs

1 cup whole milk

1 cup shredded part-skim mozzarella cheese (4 ounces)

1 cup grated Parmesan cheese (3 ounces)

1 container (15 ounces) part-skim ricotta cheese

4 ounces sliced pepperoni, cut into slivers (1 cup)

1 package (10 ounces) frozen peas

½ teaspoon salt

¼ teaspoon ground black pepper

1. In large saucepot, cook pasta as label directs.

2. Meanwhile, preheat oven to 375°F. Grease 3- to 3½-quart casserole (about 2 inches deep) or 13" by 9" glass baking dish.

3. In large bowl, with wire whisk, lightly beat eggs. Stir in milk, mozzarella, Parmesan, ricotta, pepperoni, frozen peas, salt, and pepper until well combined.

4. Drain rigatoni. Add rigatoni to cheese mixture and toss to coat. Transfer rigatoni mixture to prepared casserole. Bake, uncovered, 20 to 25 minutes or until edges are golden and center is almost set. Let stand 5 minutes before serving.

EACH SERVING About 675 calories | 39 g protein | 70 g carbohydrate | 26 g total fat (13 g saturated) | 134 mg cholesterol | 1,280 mg sodium.

Tomato and Cheese Pie

A savory custard pie that bakes right in the pie plate—with no crust!

PREP 20 minutes **BAKE** 30 minutes **MAKES** 6 main-dish servings

1 container (15 ounces) part-skim ricotta cheese

4 large eggs

¼ cup grated Parmesan cheese

¾ teaspoon salt plus additional for sprinkling

⅛ teaspoon coarsely ground black pepper plus additional for sprinkling

¼ cup low-fat (1%) milk

1 tablespoon cornstarch

1 cup packed fresh basil leaves, chopped

1 pound ripe tomatoes (about 3 medium), thinly sliced

1. Preheat oven to 375°F. In large bowl, with wire whisk or fork, beat ricotta, eggs, Parmesan, salt, and pepper until blended.

2. In cup, stir milk and cornstarch until smooth; whisk into cheese mixture. Stir in basil.

3. Pour mixture into 9-inch glass or ceramic pie plate. Arrange tomatoes on top, overlapping if necessary. Sprinkle tomatoes with salt and pepper. Bake pie 30 to 35 minutes or until lightly browned around edge and center is puffed.

EACH SERVING About 190 calories | 15 g protein | 10 g carbohydrate | 10 g total fat (5 g saturated) | 167 mg cholesterol | 515 mg sodium.

Chili Potpie with Cheddar-Biscuit Crust

The cornmeal-and-Cheddar crust adds an old-fashioned crowning touch to spicy beef chili—an irresistible combination. Serve with a green salad.

PREP 30 minutes **BAKE** I hour 45 minutes **MAKES** 6 main-dish servings

- I tablespoon plus 3 teaspoons olive oil
- I pound boneless beef chuck, cut into ½-inch pieces
- I medium onion, chopped
- 2 garlic cloves, minced
- I tablespoon chili powder
- I teaspoon ground coriander
- ½ teaspoon salt
- ½ teaspoon ground cumin
- I can (16 ounces) whole tomatoes in puree
- I can (4 to 4½ ounces) chopped mild green chiles
- I tablespoon dark brown sugar
- I tablespoon tomato paste
- I can (15 to 16 ounces) pink beans
- ¼ cup chopped fresh cilantro leaves
- Cheddar-Biscuit Crust (recipe follows)
- 2 teaspoons milk
- green onions for garnish (optional)

I. In 5-quart Dutch oven or saucepot, heat 1 tablespoon olive oil over medium-high heat until hot. Add half the beef, and cook until browned and juices evaporate. Transfer beef to small bowl. Repeat with remaining beef and 2 teaspoons olive oil.

2. Add remaining 1 teaspoon olive oil to Dutch oven. Reduce heat to medium. Add onion and cook 10 minutes or until tender and golden. Add garlic; cook 2 minutes, stirring. Add chili powder, coriander, salt, and cumin; cook 1 minute, stirring.

3. Add tomatoes with their puree, breaking up tomatoes with side of spoon. Add chiles with their juice, brown sugar, tomato paste, beef with any accumulated juices in bowl, and ¼ *cup water*; heat to boiling over high heat. Reduce heat to low; cover and simmer 30 minutes, stirring occasionally.

4. Rinse and drain beans. Add beans; heat to boiling over high heat. Reduce heat to low; cover and simmer 30 to 45 minutes longer, until beef is very tender. Stir in cilantro.

5. Preheat oven to 425°F. Meanwhile, prepare Cheddar-Biscuit Crust.

6. Spoon hot chili mixture into deep 2-quart casserole or 9-inch deep-dish pie plate. Top with biscuit crust, tucking in edge to fit. With tip of knife, cut out 5 oval openings in crust to allow steam to escape during baking. (Do not just make slits, they will close up as crust bakes.) Brush crust with milk.

7. Place sheet of foil underneath casserole; crimp foil edges to form a rim to catch any drips during baking. Bake pie 20 minutes or until crust is browned. Cool slightly.

8. Garnish each serving with green onions if you like.

CHEDDAR-BISCUIT CRUST In a medium bowl, mix **1 cup all-purpose flour**, ⅓ **cup shredded sharp Cheddar cheese**, ¼ **cup yellow cornmeal**, **2 teaspoons baking powder**, and ½ **teaspoon salt**. With pastry blender or 2 knives used scissor-fashion, cut in **3 tablespoons cold butter or margarine** until mixture resembles coarse crumbs. Stir in ½ **cup milk**; quickly mix just until a soft dough forms and leaves side of bowl. Turn dough onto lightly floured surface; gently knead about 5 strokes to mix thoroughly. With floured rolling pin, roll dough into a round 1 inch larger in diameter than top of casserole.

EACH SERVING About 515 calories | 24 g protein | 45 g carbohydrate | 27 g total fat (8 g saturated) | 58 mg cholesterol | 1,320 mg sodium.

Savory Tomato Tart

A dramatically beautiful main dish. We used a yellow tomato for more color, but you can use all red if you prefer.

PREP 45 minutes   **BAKE/BROIL** 30 minutes   **MAKES** 6 main-dish servings

Pastry for 11-inch Tart (recipe follows)

1 tablespoon olive oil

3 medium onions, thinly sliced

½ teaspoon salt

1 package (3½ ounces) goat cheese

1 ripe medium yellow tomato (8 ounces), cut into ¼-inch-thick slices

2 ripe medium red tomatoes (8 ounces each), cut into ¼-inch-thick slices

½ teaspoon coarsely ground black pepper

¼ cup kalamata olives, pitted and chopped

1. Preheat oven to 425°F. Prepare Pastry for 11-inch Tart and use to line tart pan as directed. Line tart shell with foil; fill with pie weights or dry beans. Bake 15 minutes. Remove foil with weights. Bake until golden, 5 to 10 minutes longer. If shell puffs up during baking, gently press it down with back of spoon.

2. Meanwhile, in nonstick 12-inch skillet, heat oil over medium heat. Add onions and ¼ teaspoon salt; cook, stirring frequently, until very tender, about 20 minutes.

3. Turn oven control to broil. Spread onions over bottom of tart shell and crumble half of goat cheese on top. Arrange yellow and red tomatoes, alternating colors, in concentric circles over onion-cheese mixture. Sprinkle with remaining ¼ teaspoon salt and ground pepper. Crumble remaining goat cheese on top of tart.

4. Place tart on rack in broiling pan. Place pan in broiler about 7 inches from heat source. Broil until cheese has melted and tomatoes are heated through, 6 to 8 minutes. Sprinkle with olives.

PASTRY FOR 11-INCH TART In large bowl, combine **1½ cups all-purpose flour** and ½ **teaspoon salt**. With pastry blender or 2 knives used scissor-fashion, cut in ½ **cup cold butter or margarine (1 stick),** cut into pieces and **2 tablespoons vegetable shortening** until mixture resembles coarse crumbs. Sprinkle in **3 to 4 tablespoons ice water**, 1 tablespoon at a time, mixing lightly with fork after each addition, until dough is just moist enough to hold together. Shape dough into disk; wrap in plastic wrap. Refrigerate 30 minutes or up to overnight. (If chilled overnight, let stand 30 minutes at room temperature before rolling.) On lightly floured surface, with floured rolling pin, roll dough into 14-inch round. Ease dough into 11-inch tart pan with removable bottom. Fold overhang in and press dough against side of pan so it extends ⅛ inch above rim. Refrigerate or freeze until firm, 10 to 15 minutes. Fill and bake as directed in recipe.

EACH SERVING About 420 calories | 8 g protein | 33 g carbohydrate | 29 g total fat (15 g saturated) | 54 mg cholesterol | 755 mg sodium.

Couscous Paella

A box of couscous makes paella quick enough for a weeknight.

PREP 10 minutes **COOK** 10 minutes **MAKES** 4 main-dish servings

1 can (14½ ounces) chicken broth

1 package (10 ounces) couscous (1½ cups)

1 package (10 ounces) frozen peas

2 teaspoons olive oil

1 red or green pepper, diced

2 ounces low-fat kielbasa (smoked Polish sausage), sliced

12 ounces skinless, boneless chicken breast, cut into 1-inch pieces

1 garlic clove, crushed with garlic press

½ teaspoon salt

¼ teaspoon dried thyme

¼ teaspoon coarsely ground black pepper

1½ cups cherry tomatoes, each cut in half

1. In 3-quart saucepan, heat chicken broth and ¼ *cup water* to boiling over high heat. Remove saucepan from heat; stir in couscous and frozen peas. Cover saucepan and let stand 5 minutes or until ready to use.

2. Meanwhile, in nonstick 12-inch skillet, heat olive oil over medium-high heat until hot. Add red or green pepper and kielbasa and cook 5 minutes, stirring occasionally. Add chicken, garlic, salt, thyme, and black pepper, and cook until chicken loses its pink color throughout, about 5 minutes, stirring occasionally. Remove skillet from heat and stir in cherry-tomato halves.

3. Fluff the couscous with fork; add to the chicken mixture in skillet, and toss gently until combined.

EACH SERVING About 520 calories | 38 g protein | 73 g carbohydrate | 8 g total fat (1 g saturated) | 50 mg cholesterol | 725 mg sodium.

Tuna-Melt Casserole

If you enjoy diner tuna-melt sandwiches, you'll love this. We've added tomatoes and broccoli for flavor, color, and vitamins.

⏱ **PREP** 40 minutes   **BAKE** 20 minutes   **MAKES** 6 main-dish servings

1 package (16 ounces) corkscrew or medium shell pasta

salt

3 cups broccoli flowerets

2 tablespoons butter or margarine

2 tablespoons all-purpose flour

¼ teaspoon coarsely ground black pepper

4 cups reduced-fat (2%) milk

4 ounces Swiss cheese, shredded (1 cup)

1 can (12 ounces) chunk light tuna in water, drained and flaked

2 medium tomatoes, cut into ¼-inch-thick slices

1. Preheat oven to 400°F. In large saucepot, cook pasta in *boiling salted water* 5 minutes; add broccoli to pasta and cook another 5 minutes or until broccoli is tender and pasta is al dente. Drain well and return to saucepot; set aside.

2. Meanwhile, in 3-quart saucepan, melt butter over low heat. Stir in flour, ¾ teaspoon salt, and pepper until blended and cook, stirring, 1 minute. Gradually stir in milk; increase heat to medium-high and cook, stirring occasionally, until mixture thickens and boils. Boil 1 minute, stirring frequently. Remove saucepan from heat and stir in ½ cup Swiss cheese until blended.

3. Add cheese sauce and tuna to pasta and broccoli in saucepot; toss until evenly mixed. Transfer mixture to shallow 3½-quart casserole or 13" by 9" glass baking dish. Arrange tomato slices on top, overlapping if necessary. Sprinkle with remaining ½ cup cheese.

4. Cover baking dish with foil and bake 20 minutes or until hot and bubbly.

EACH SERVING About 570 calories | **39 g protein** | **71 g carbohydrate** | 14 g total fat (6 g saturated) | **29 mg cholesterol** | **755 mg sodium.**

Turkey Potpie with Cornmeal Crust

Treat your family to the ultimate in comfort food—tender turkey and veggies in a velvety sauce nestled under a golden crust.

🕐 **PREP** 30 minutes   **BAKE** 35 minutes   **MAKES** 10 main-dish servings

1 tablespoon vegetable oil

1 medium rutabaga (1 pound), peeled and cut into ½-inch pieces

3 carrots, peeled and cut into ½-inch pieces

1 large onion (12 ounces), chopped

1 pound all-purpose potatoes (3 medium), peeled and cut into ½-inch pieces

2 large stalks celery, chopped

¾ teaspoon salt

1 pound cooked turkey or chicken, cut into ½-inch pieces (4 cups)

1 package (10 ounces) frozen peas

1 can (14½ ounces) chicken broth or 1¾ cups Chicken Broth (page 9)

1 cup milk

¼ cup all-purpose flour

¼ teaspoon ground black pepper

⅛ teaspoon dried thyme

Cornmeal Crust (recipe follows)

1 large egg, beaten

1. In nonstick 12-inch skillet, heat oil over medium-high heat; add rutabaga, carrots, and onion and cook 10 minutes. Stir in potatoes, celery, and ½ teaspoon salt; cook, stirring frequently, until rutabaga is tender-crisp, about 10 minutes longer. Spoon into 13" by 9" baking dish; add turkey and peas.

2. In 2-quart saucepan, heat broth to boiling. Meanwhile, in small bowl, blend milk and flour until smooth. Stir milk mixture into broth; add pepper, thyme, and remaining ¼ teaspoon salt. Heat to boiling over high heat, stirring. Stir sauce into turkey-vegetable mixture in baking dish.

3. Prepare the Cornmeal Crust. Preheat oven to 425°F.

4. On lightly floured surface, with floured rolling pin, roll dough into rectangle 4 inches larger than top of baking dish. Arrange dough rectangle over filling; trim edge, leaving 1-inch overhang. Fold overhang under; flute. Brush crust with some egg. If desired, reroll trimmings; cut into

decorative shapes to garnish top of pie. Brush dough cutouts with egg. Cut several slits in crust to allow steam to escape during baking.

5. Place potpie on foil-lined cookie sheet to catch any overflow during baking. Bake potpie until crust is golden brown and filling is hot and bubbling, 35 to 40 minutes. During last 10 minutes of baking, cover edges of crust with foil to prevent overbrowning.

CORNMEAL CRUST In large bowl, combine **1½ cups all-purpose flour,** **¼ cup cornmeal,** and **¾ teaspoon salt.** With pastry blender or 2 knives used scissor-fashion, cut in **⅔ cup vegetable shortening** until mixture resembles coarse crumbs. Sprinkle **6 to 7 tablespoons cold water,** 1 tablespoon at a time, over flour mixture, mixing with fork after each addition until dough is just moist enough to hold together.

EACH SERVING About 416 calories | **21 g protein** | **42 g carbohydrate** | **18 g total fat (5 g saturated)** | **60 mg cholesterol** | **644 mg sodium.**

Linguine with Tuna and Broccoli

In our delicious variation on linguine with clam sauce, we have tuna cooked with garlic and white wine stand in for the clams.

🍲 **PREP** 5 minutes   **COOK** 10 minutes   **MAKES** 4 main-dish servings

2 packages (9 ounces each) fresh (refrigerated) linguine

2 packages (10 ounces each) frozen broccoli cuts

2 teaspoons salt

2 tablespoons olive oil

3 garlic cloves, crushed with garlic press

¼ teaspoon crushed red pepper

¼ cup dry white wine

1 can (12 ounces) tuna packed in water, drained and flaked

1. In large saucepot, heat *5 quarts water* to boiling over high heat. Add pasta, broccoli, and 2 teaspoons salt; cook 2 to 3 minutes or until linguine and broccoli are tender.

2. Meanwhile, in nonstick 10-inch skillet, heat oil over medium-high heat until hot. Add garlic and crushed red pepper, and cook 1 minute, stirring. Add wine and heat to boiling; boil 1 minute, stirring. Stir in tuna and cook 30 seconds.

3. When linguine is cooked, remove *½ cup pasta cooking water*; reserve. Drain linguine and broccoli and return to saucepot. Add tuna mixture, ½ teaspoon salt, and reserved pasta cooking water; toss until well mixed.

EACH SERVING About 595 calories | 36 g protein | 79 g carbohydrate | 15 g total fat (3 g saturated) | 174 mg cholesterol | 800 mg sodium.

Thai Pasta with Shrimp

Delicate angel hair pasta absorbs sauce quickly, so put this on plates as soon as it's tossed. Serve with lime wedges if you like.

🕐 **PREP** 15 minutes   **COOK** 15 minutes   **MAKES** 6 main-dish servings

1 package (16 ounces) angel hair pasta

2 teaspoons curry powder

1 can (14 ounces) light coconut milk (not cream of coconut)

1 teaspoon salt

⅛ teaspoon coarsely ground black pepper

1 pound medium shrimp, shelled and deveined with tail part of shell left on (page 13)

1 cup loosely packed fresh cilantro leaves

1. In large saucepot, cook pasta as label directs.

2. Meanwhile, in 10-inch skillet, cook curry powder over medium heat 2 minutes, stirring frequently. Stir in coconut milk, salt, and pepper until blended; heat to boiling over high heat. Add shrimp; reduce heat to medium. Cover and cook 2 minutes or until shrimp just turn opaque throughout.

3. Drain pasta. In large bowl, toss pasta with shrimp mixture and cilantro.

EACH SERVING About 410 calories | 23 g protein | 59 g carbohydrate | 8 g total fat (4 g saturated) | 95 mg cholesterol | 550 mg sodium.

Greek Pasta Bowl with Shrimp

Oregano and feta cheese—two staples of Greek cooking—flavor this dish. For an even speedier prep time, substitute pre-shelled and deveined frozen raw shrimp for the fresh.

PREP 15 minutes **COOK** 15 minutes **MAKES** 6 main-dish servings

1 package (16 ounces) gemelli or fusilli pasta

2 tablespoons olive oil

1 pound medium shrimp, shelled and deveined (page 13)

2 garlic cloves, crushed with garlic press

1 tablespoon fresh oregano leaves, minced, or ½ teaspoon dried oregano

½ teaspoon salt

¼ teaspoon ground black pepper

2 bunches green onions, thinly sliced

3 medium tomatoes (about 1 pound), coarsely chopped

2 packages (4 ounces each) crumbled feta cheese (about 2 cups)

fresh oregano sprigs for garnish

1. In large saucepot, cook pasta as label directs.

2. Meanwhile, in nonstick 12-inch skillet, heat oil over medium-high heat until hot. Add shrimp, garlic, oregano, salt, and pepper and cook 1 minute, stirring. Add green onions and cook 2 minutes or just until shrimp turn opaque throughout. Stir in tomatoes.

3. Drain pasta; return to saucepot. Add shrimp mixture and feta; toss well to combine. Garnish each serving with the fresh oregano sprigs.

EACH SERVING About 515 calories | 29 g protein | 65 g carbohydrate | 15 g total fat (7 g saturated) | 127 mg cholesterol | 815 mg sodium.

Shrimp and Orzo in Feta-Tomato Sauce

Orzo is the Italian word for barley, but it's used here in its more common form as a rice-shaped pasta. Serve with a side salad.

PREP 15 minutes   **COOK** 15 minutes   **MAKES** 4 main-dish servings

1 box (16 ounces) orzo pasta

1 tablespoon olive oil

1 bunch green onions, cut into 1-inch pieces

1 large garlic clove, finely chopped

¼ teaspoon dried oregano

⅛ teaspoon crushed red pepper

1 can (28 ounces) plum tomatoes in juice

1 pound medium shrimp, shelled and deveined (page 13)

4 ounces feta cheese, crumbled (1 cup)

Salt

1. In large saucepot, cook pasta as label directs.

2. Meanwhile, in 12-inch skillet, heat olive oil over medium heat until hot. Add green onions and garlic and cook 1 minute or until fragrant, stirring. Stir in oregano and red pepper.

3. Add tomatoes with their juice, breaking up tomatoes with side of spoon. Cook, uncovered, 2 to 3 minutes or until liquid thickens slightly.

4. Stir in shrimp; cover and cook 3 to 5 minutes or until shrimp turn opaque throughout, stirring once. Stir feta into skillet; add salt to taste.

5. To serve, drain orzo; spoon into four shallow bowls. Top with shrimp and sauce.

EACH SERVING About 670 calories | 40 g protein | 97 g carbohydrate | 13 g total fat (5 g saturated) | 165 mg cholesterol | 825 mg sodium.

Vegetarian Phyllo Pizza

Phyllo replaces the traditional pie dough and makes for a refreshingly light pizza. Since you won't have to wait around for the dough to rise, this is great as a weeknight meal. Serve with a side salad.

PREP 10 minutes   **BAKE** 15 minutes   **MAKES** 4 main-dish servings

6 sheets (17" by 12" each) fresh or frozen (thawed) phyllo

2 tablespoons margarine or butter, melted

4 ounces soft, mild goat cheese such as Montrachet

1 jar (6 ounces) marinated artichoke hearts, drained and cut into chunks

1½ cups grape or cherry tomatoes, each cut in half

1. Preheat oven to 450°F. Place 1 sheet of phyllo on ungreased large cookie sheet; brush with some melted margarine. Repeat layering with remaining phyllo and margarine; do not brush top layer.

2. Crumble goat cheese over phyllo; top with artichokes and tomatoes. Bake pizza 12 to 15 minutes or until golden brown around the edges.

3. Transfer pizza to large cutting board. With pizza cutter or knife, cut pizza lengthwise in half, then cut each half crosswise into 4 pieces.

EACH SERVING About 245 calories | 8 g protein | 20 g carbohydrate | 16 g total fat (6 g saturated) | 13 mg cholesterol | 405 mg sodium.

Q: When a recipe calls for goat cheese, how do I know which kind to buy?

A: In general, the creamier the cheese, the milder it tastes. "Older" or aged goat cheeses usually have a rind and a tart bite. We most often call for fairly mellow varieties that don't overpower the other flavors in savory pies and quiches.

Goat cheese (or *chèvre*, French for "goat") tends to be tarter than cow's-milk cheeses like Cheddar and sheep's-milk products like Pecorino Romano. And as chèvre ages, it gets sharper and more crumbly. We like white, creamy varieties such as **Montrachet**—a log-shaped cheese from the Burgundy region of France. But other unripened kinds, in shapes like pyramids and disks, work well too, including **Ste. Maure**, **Chabais**, and **Bûche**. Ripened chèvre is nice served on a platter with other cheeses or tossed with baby greens. (The distinctive rind doesn't mean the cheese is past its prime; the outer layer is part of the natural aging process, and you can eat it or cut it off.)

You'll also see goat cheeses covered with herbs, peppers, or grape leaves, which add flavor. Other kinds are coated with ash, to dry out the exterior of the cheese, inhibit the growth of mold, and encourage ripening. Commercial ash is now made from milk, slat, and wood ash, and is completely edible—and tasteless.

Penne with Three Cheeses and Porcini Mushrooms

You won't miss the meat here, as the porcini mushrooms lend a meaty, slightly nutty flavor to this hearty vegetarian dish. Serve with a green salad.

PREP 30 minutes **COOK** 30 minutes **MAKES** 8 main-dish servings

- 1 package (16 ounces) penne rigate or ziti pasta
- 1 cup water
- 1 ounce dried porcini mushrooms (about 1 cup)
- 2 tablespoons margarine or butter
- 1 medium onion, finely chopped
- 1 teaspoon fresh thyme leaves, chopped

- 3 tablespoons all-purpose flour
- 2½ cups reduced-fat (2%) milk
- ⅛ teaspoon ground nutmeg
- 1 teaspoon salt
- ¼ teaspoon ground black pepper
- 4 ounces Fontina cheese, cubed
- 1 cup part-skim ricotta cheese
- 1 cup freshly grated Parmesan cheese

1. In large saucepot, cook pasta 2 minutes less than label directs. Drain and return to pot.

2. Meanwhile, preheat oven to 375°F. In microwave-safe 4-cup liquid measuring cup or medium bowl, heat water in microwave oven on High 1½ to 2 minutes or until boiling. Stir in porcini mushrooms; let stand 15 minutes. With slotted spoon, remove porcini; rinse to remove any grit. Finely chop and set aside. Strain soaking liquid through sieve lined with paper towel and set aside.

3. In 4-quart saucepan, melt margarine over medium heat. Add onion and cook 8 to 9 minutes or until tender and lightly browned, stirring occasionally. Stir in porcini and thyme.

4. Sprinkle flour over onion mixture in saucepan; cook 1 minute, stirring. Whisk in milk, mushroom liquid, nutmeg, salt, and pepper. Heat to boiling over medium-high heat; cook 2 to 3 minutes or until mixture thickens slightly, stirring frequently.

5. Add porcini sauce to pasta in saucepot. Stir in Fontina, ricotta, and ½ cup Parmesan until combined. Spoon pasta into 3-quart ceramic baking dish; sprinkle with remaining Parmesan. Bake 30 minutes or until center is hot and top is golden.

EACH SERVING About 465 calories | 24 g protein | 55 g carbohydrate | 16 g total fat (8 g saturated) | 42 mg cholesterol | 765 mg sodium.

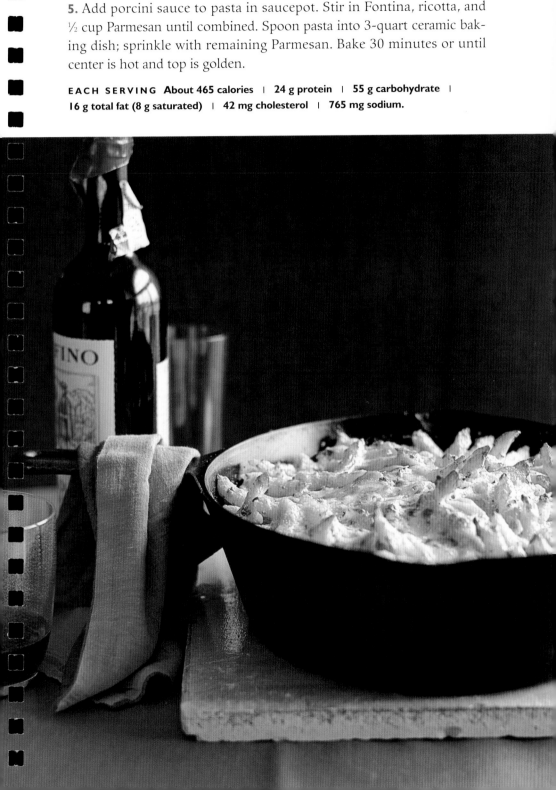

Baked Pasta with Butternut Squash

To save some prep time for this recipe, look for cut-up butternut squash in your produce department (see photo on page 107).

PREP 45 minutes **COOK** 30 minutes
MAKES About 12 cups or 6 main-dish servings

4 ounces pancetta, cut into
¼-inch dice

5 shallots, sliced (about 1 cup)

¼ teaspoon ground black pepper

2 teaspoons olive oil

1 butternut squash (about 2
pounds), peeled, seeded, and cut
into ¾-inch chunks

1 container (10 ounces) Brussels
sprouts, each cut into quarters

10 medium sage leaves, chopped
(about 3 tablespoons)

1 can (14 to 14½ ounces) chicken
broth (1¾ cups) plus whole leaves
for garnish

1 package (16 ounces) cavatappi or
corkscrew pasta

1½ cups reduced-fat (2%) milk

1 cup freshly grated Parmesan
cheese (about 3 ounces)

Fried sage leaves for garnish
(see note)

1. Preheat oven to 375°F. In nonstick 12-inch skillet, cook pancetta over medium heat about 10 minutes or until browned, stirring occasionally. With slotted spoon, transfer pancetta to medium bowl. In same skillet, cook shallots with pepper about 5 minutes or until golden, stirring frequently. Transfer shallots to bowl with pancetta.

2. In same skillet, heat olive oil over medium heat until hot; add squash and cook, covered, 10 minutes, stirring often. Add Brussels sprouts, sage, and broth; cook, covered, 10 to 12 minutes or until vegetables are tender and most of liquid is absorbed.

3. Meanwhile, in large saucepot, cook pasta 2 minutes less than label directs. Drain and return to saucepot.

4. Stir milk into skillet with squash and heat through. Add squash mixture, pancetta mixture, and ¾ cup Parmesan to pasta in saucepot; toss until well mixed. Spoon pasta into 3-quart ceramic baking dish and sprinkle with bread crumbs and remaining Parmesan. Bake 30 minutes or until center is hot and top is golden. Garnish with fried sage leaves.

Note: To make fried sage leaves: Heat ¼ cup olive oil in 10-inch skillet over medium heat until hot. Add ½ cup sage leaves, rinsed and patted dry; cook about 1 minute or until crisp, turning leaves over once and being careful not to burn them. Remove with slotted spoon; drain on paper towels.

EACH SERVING About 600 calories | 25 g protein | 87 g carbohydrate | 17 g total fat (8 g saturated) | 27 mg cholesterol | 760 mg sodium.

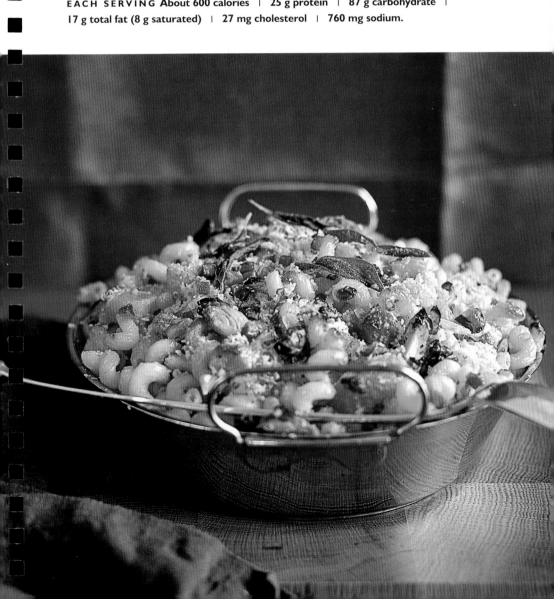

Lo Mein with Tofu, Snow Peas, and Carrots

Using packaged soup mix and bottled stir-fry sauce to give you a head start, this balanced meatless meal is practically done before you've started.

PREP 15 minutes   COOK 15 minutes   MAKES 4 main-dish servings

2 packages (3 ounces each) Oriental-flavor ramen noodle soup mix

2 teaspoons vegetable oil

1 package (14 to 15 ounces) extra-firm tofu, patted dry and diced

6 ounces snow peas, strings removed and each cut diagonally in half (about 2 cups)

3 green onions, cut into 2-inch pieces

1½ cups shredded carrots (about half 10-ounce package)

½ cup bottled stir-fry sauce

3 ounces fresh bean sprouts (about 1 cup), rinsed and drained

1. Heat covered 4-quart saucepan of water to boiling over high heat. Add ramen noodles (reserve flavor packets) and cook 2 minutes. Drain noodles, reserving 1/4 cup noodle cooking water.

2. Meanwhile, in nonstick 12-inch skillet, heat oil over medium-high heat until very hot. Add tofu and cook 5 to 6 minutes or until lightly browned, stirring occasionally. Add snow peas and green onions to skillet; cook 3 to 5 minutes or until vegetables are tender-crisp, stirring frequently. Stir in carrots, stir-fry sauce, and contents of 1 flavor packet to taste (depending on salt level of sauce), and cook 2 minutes or until carrots are tender. (Discard remaining flavor packet or save for another use.)

3. Reserve some bean sprouts for garnish. Add noodles, reserved noodle water, and remaining bean sprouts to skillet; cook 1 minute to blend flavors, stirring. Sprinkle with reserved bean sprouts to serve.

EACH SERVING About 375 calories | 18 g protein | 47 g carbohydrate | 12 g total fat (3 g saturated) | 0 mg cholesterol | 1,485 mg sodium.

Salads & Sandwiches

Falafel Sandwiches
recipe on page 166

Taco Salad

Better than a taco! For quick assembly, have all the ingredients chopped and ready to go.

PREP 30 minutes **COOK** 20 minutes **MAKES** 6 main-dish servings

2 teaspoons vegetable oil

1 medium onion, chopped

1 garlic clove, finely chopped

2 tablespoons chili powder

1 teaspoon ground cumin

1 pound ground beef chuck

1 can (8 ounces) tomato sauce

1 head iceberg lettuce, cut into quarters, cored, and very thinly sliced

1 large ripe tomato (10 ounces), finely chopped

1 ripe avocado, peeled, pitted, and chopped

4 ounces sharp Cheddar cheese, shredded (1 cup)

3 tablespoons sour cream

1 cup loosely packed small cilantro leaves

½ bag (5 ounces) tortilla chips

1. In 10-inch skillet, heat oil over medium heat. Add onion and cook, stirring occasionally, until tender, about 5 minutes. Stir in garlic, chili powder, and cumin and cook 30 seconds. Add ground beef, stirring to break up lumps with side of spoon; cook until no longer pink, about 5 minutes. Stir in tomato sauce and cook 5 minutes longer.

2. Divide lettuce among dinner plates. Spoon warm beef mixture on top of lettuce. Sprinkle with tomato, avocado, and Cheddar. Top each with some sour cream; sprinkle with cilantro. Tuck tortilla chips around edge of each plate.

EACH SERVING About 506 calories | 22 g protein | 21 g carbohydrate | 38 g total fat (15 g saturated) | 87 mg cholesterol | 504 mg sodium.

GH Test Kitchen Tip

For a heartier dish, add drained canned beans or corn to the beef mixture.

Cajun Chicken Salad with Green Grapes

Enjoy a great combination of poached chicken, red pepper, and juicy grapes in a spicy, creamy dressing. We toasted the thyme and paprika to add extra flavor to the dressing and used reduced-fat sour cream to lower the fat.

PREP 25 minutes   **COOK** 20 minutes   **MAKES** 8 main-dish servings

I lemon, thinly sliced

I bay leaf

½ teaspoon whole black peppercorns

½ teaspoon dried thyme

6 medium skinless, boneless chicken-breast halves (1¾ pounds)

¾ teaspoon paprika

⅓ cup light mayonnaise

⅓ cup reduced-fat sour cream

¾ teaspoon salt

¼ teaspoon coarsely ground black pepper

⅛ teaspoon ground nutmeg

3 cups green grapes (about 12 ounces), each cut in half

I large red pepper, cut into ½-inch dice

½ cup loosely packed fresh parsley leaves, chopped

¼ cup thinly sliced red onion

I large pickled jalapeño chile, minced

1. In 12-inch skillet, heat *1 inch water* with lemon slices, bay leaf, peppercorns, and ¼ teaspoon thyme to boiling over high heat. Add chicken; reduce heat to low and simmer 12 to 14 minutes, turning chicken over halfway through cooking, until chicken just loses its pink color throughout. With slotted spoon or tongs, transfer chicken from skillet to cutting board; cool slightly until easy to handle. Cut chicken into ¾-inch pieces.

2. Discard poaching liquid and wipe skillet dry. Add paprika and remaining ¼ teaspoon thyme to skillet; toast over medium-low heat, stirring, 2 minutes.

3. Transfer paprika mixture to large bowl; stir in mayonnaise, sour cream, salt, pepper, and nutmeg until blended. Add chicken, grapes, red pepper, parsley, onion, and jalapeño; toss until evenly coated. Serve salad warm, or cover and refrigerate until ready to serve.

EACH SERVING About 200 calories | 24 g protein | 16 g carbohydrate | 4 g total fat (1 g saturated) | 64 mg cholesterol | 380 mg sodium.

Curried Chicken and Mango Salad

Precooked chicken from the deli or supermarket makes our salad a cinch. The recipe can easily be doubled if you need to feed a crowd.

PREP 20 minutes   **MAKES** 4 main-dish servings

1 store-bought rotisserie chicken
  (about 2 pounds)

¼ cup plain low-fat yogurt

¼ cup light mayonnaise

2 tablespoons mango chutney,
  chopped

1 tablespoon fresh lime juice

1 teaspoon curry powder

1 ripe large mango, peeled and diced

1 medium stalk celery, diced

1 medium Granny Smith apple,
  cored and diced

½ cup loosely packed fresh cilantro
  leaves, chopped

1 head leaf lettuce, separated and
  rinsed

cilantro leaves for garnish

1. Remove skin from chicken; discard. With fingers, pull chicken meat into 1-inch pieces. (You should have about 3 cups, or about ¾ pound meat.)

2. In large bowl, mix yogurt, mayonnaise, chutney, lime juice, and curry powder until combined. Stir in chicken, mango, celery, apple, and cilantro until well coated. Serve salad on bed of lettuce leaves. Garnish with cilantro leaves.

EACH SERVING About 310 calories | 32 g protein | 25 g carbohydrate | 9 g total fat (2 g saturated) | 95 mg cholesterol | 255 mg sodium.

Warm Chicken and Spinach Salad

A perfect dinner on the lighter side—sautéed chicken tenders and asparagus served on a bed of baby spinach, drizzled with mustard vinaigrette.

🕐 **PREP** 15 minutes **COOK** 20 minutes **MAKES** 4 main-dish servings

I bag (about 6 ounces) baby spinach

3 teaspoons plus I tablespoon olive oil

I pound medium asparagus, trimmed and cut diagonally into 1½-inch pieces

I large shallot, thinly sliced

I pound chicken-breast tenders

½ teaspoon salt

¼ teaspoon coarsely ground black pepper

I tablespoon balsamic vinegar

I tablespoon fresh lemon juice

½ teaspoon Dijon mustard

¼ teaspoon sugar

1. Place spinach leaves on large platter and set aside.

2. In nonstick 12-inch skillet, heat 2 teaspoons olive oil over medium-high heat until hot. Add asparagus and shallot, and cook 5 minutes or until golden, stirring occasionally. Reduce heat to medium; add *2 tablespoons water* and cook, covered, 5 minutes longer or until asparagus is tender, stirring occasionally. Spoon asparagus mixture over spinach.

3. Increase heat to medium-high. In same skillet, in 1 teaspoon olive oil, cook chicken with ¼ teaspoon salt and ⅛ teaspoon pepper until it loses its pink color throughout, 5 minutes, turning once.

4. Meanwhile, prepare dressing: In cup, with wire whisk or fork, mix vinegar, lemon juice, mustard, sugar, remaining 1 tablespoon olive oil, remaining ¼ teaspoon salt, and remaining ⅛ teaspoon pepper until blended.

5. Spoon chicken onto platter with spinach and asparagus. Add dressing to hot skillet and cook 30 seconds, stirring. Drizzle mixture over chicken and vegetables.

EACH SERVING About 225 calories | 30 g protein | 8 g carbohydrate | 9 g total fat (1 g saturated) | 66 mg cholesterol | 395 mg sodium.

Thai Salad

A summery blend of chicken, lettuce, fresh herbs, and crisp carrots tossed with a tangy, spicy Asian dressing. It is equally good made with either beef or shrimp in place of the chicken.

PREP 20 minutes   MAKES 4 main-dish servings

12 cups loosely packed bite-size pieces Boston lettuce (about two 6-ounce heads)

½ cup loosely packed fresh cilantro leaves

½ cup loosely packed fresh mint leaves

1 bag (10 ounces) shredded carrots

3 green onions, cut into 1-inch pieces

¼ cup fresh lime juice

2 tablespoons Asian fish sauce (see Tip, page 97)

2 tablespoons vegetable oil

1 jalapeño chile, seeded and minced

1 tablespoon grated, peeled fresh ginger

1 teaspoon sugar

12 ounces skinless, boneless, rotisserie chicken, cut into thin strips

1. In large bowl, toss lettuce with cilantro, mint, carrots, and green onions.

2. In another large bowl, with wire whisk, mix lime juice, fish sauce, oil, jalapeño, ginger, and sugar until blended.

3. To serve, add chicken to dressing in bowl; toss to coat. Add lettuce mixture; toss again.

EACH SERVING About 285 calories | 27 g protein | 14 g carbohydrate | 14 g total fat (2 g saturated) | 76 mg cholesterol | 755 mg sodium.

Couscous and Smoked-Turkey Salad

Sweet nectarines contrast nicely with the smoky flavor of the turkey in this superquick salad. If you see plums, peaches, or apricots at the farmers' market, try using them in place of the nectarines.

PREP 10 minutes **COOK** 5 minutes **MAKES** 6 main-dish servings

1 teaspoon ground cumin

1 package (10 ounces) couscous

⅓ cup dried tart cherries

3 tablespoons fresh lemon juice

2 tablespoons olive oil

1 tablespoon Dijon mustard

¾ teaspoon salt

¼ teaspoon coarsely ground black pepper

3 ripe medium nectarines, diced

4 ounces smoked turkey breast (in 1 piece), cut into ¼-inch pieces

Boston lettuce leaves

1. In 3-quart saucepan, heat cumin over medium-high heat until fragrant, 1 to 3 minutes. In saucepan with cumin, prepare couscous as label directs, adding cherries but no salt or butter.

2. In large bowl, with wire whisk or fork, mix lemon juice, olive oil, mustard, salt, and pepper until dressing is blended.

3. Toss warm couscous mixture, diced nectarines, and turkey with dressing.

4. Spoon couscous onto large platter lined with Boston lettuce leaves.

EACH SERVING About 300 calories | 11 g protein | 51 g carbohydrate | 6 g total fat (1 g saturated) | 3 mg cholesterol | 470 mg sodium.

Shrimp and Tomato Summer Salad

This Greek-inspired salad is best when tomatoes are at their summer peak and fresh herbs are plentiful. In the off-seasons, grape tomatoes, cut in halves, make a nice substitute.

PREP 25 minutes **MAKES** 6 main-dish servings

2 tablespoons olive oil

2 tablespoons red wine vinegar

¾ teaspoon salt

¼ teaspoon coarsely ground black pepper

½ cup loosely packed fresh parsley leaves, chopped

¼ cup loosely packed fresh mint leaves, thinly sliced

I pound shelled and deveined cooked large shrimp (page 13)

4 ripe large tomatoes (about 2½ pounds), cut into 1-inch chunks

I English (seedless) cucumber or 4 Kirby cucumbers, cut lengthwise into quarters, then cut crosswise into 1-inch chunks

I small red onion, diced

½ cup crumbled feta cheese (about 2 ounces)

1. In serving bowl, whisk together olive oil, vinegar, salt, and pepper; stir in parsley and mint.

2. Add shrimp, tomatoes, cucumber, and onion to dressing in bowl; stir to combine. Sprinkle salad with feta to serve. Serve at room temperature or cover and refrigerate to serve later.

EACH MAIN-DISH SERVING About 200 calories | 20 g protein | 13 g carbohydrate | 8 g total fat (2 g saturated) | 156 mg cholesterol | 585 mg sodium.

Best Tuna Salad

You can enjoy this simple family favorite two ways—on a sandwich or on a bed of salad greens. For a change of pace, try one of our three tasty variations.

🕑 **PREP** 15 minutes **MAKES** 1¼ cups or 2 main-dish servings

1 can (6 ounces) chunk-light tuna packed in water, drained

¼ cup finely chopped celery

3 tablespoons light mayonnaise

2 teaspoons fresh lemon juice

baguette or other favorite bread (optional)

In small bowl, with fork, combine all ingredients except baguette. Cover and refrigerate if not serving right away. Serve on a baguette if you like.

EACH SERVING WITHOUT BREAD About 170 calories | 19 g protein | 1 g carbohydrate | 11 g total fat (3 g saturated) | 30 mg cholesterol | 415 mg sodium.

CURRIED TUNA Prepare Best Tuna Salad as above. Stir in ½ **cup finely chopped Granny Smith apple** and **1 teaspoon curry powder**. Serve on raisin-walnut or sourdough bread if you like. Makes about 1½ cups or 2 main-dish servings.

EACH SERVING WITHOUT BREAD About 190 calories | 20 g protein | 7 g carbohydrate | 11 g total fat (3 g saturated) | 30 mg cholesterol | 415 mg sodium.

MEDITERRANEAN TUNA Prepare Best Tuna Salad as above. Stir in **2 tablespoons capers**, chopped, and ¼ **teaspoon freshly grated lemon peel**. Serve on Italian bread if you like. Makes about 1¼ cups or 2 main-dish servings.

EACH SERVING WITHOUT BREAD About 170 calories | 19 g protein | 2 g carbohydrate | 11 g total fat (3 g saturated) | 30 mg cholesterol | 730 mg sodium.

SOUTHWESTERN TUNA Prepare Best Tuna Salad as above. Stir in **2 tablespoons chop-ped fresh cilantro leaves** and **1 pickled jalapeño chile**, finely chopped. Serve rolled up in warm flour tortillas if you like. Makes about 1¼ cups or 2 main-dish servings.

EACH SERVING WITHOUT TORTILLA About 170 calories | 19 g protein | 2 g carbohydrate | 11 g total fat (3 g saturated) | 30 mg cholesterol | 510 mg sodium.

Niçoise Salad

As the story goes, the first Niçoise salad was created in eighteenth-century France, and it's been a hit ever since.

PREP 35 minutes   **COOK** 25 minutes   **MAKES** 4 main-dish servings

1 tablespoon white wine vinegar

1 tablespoon fresh lemon juice

1 tablespoon minced shallot

1 teaspoon Dijon mustard

1 teaspoon anchovy paste

¼ teaspoon sugar

¼ teaspoon coarsely ground black pepper

3 tablespoons extravirgin olive oil

1 pound medium red potatoes, not peeled, cut into ¼-inch-thick slices

8 ounces French green beans (*haricots verts*) or regular green beans, trimmed

1 head Boston lettuce, leaves separated

12 cherry tomatoes, each cut in half

1 can (12 ounces) solid white tuna packed in water, drained and flaked

2 large hard-cooked eggs, peeled and each cut into quarters

½ cup Niçoise olives

1. Prepare dressing: In small bowl, with wire whisk, mix vinegar, lemon juice, shallot, mustard, anchovy paste, sugar, and pepper until blended. In thin, steady stream, whisk in oil until blended.

2. In 3-quart saucepan, combine potatoes and *enough water to cover*; heat to boiling over high heat. Reduce heat; cover and simmer until tender, about 10 minutes. Drain.

3. Meanwhile, in 10-inch skillet, heat *1 inch water* to boiling over high heat. Add green beans; heat to boiling. Reduce heat to low and cook until tender-crisp, 6 to 8 minutes. Drain; rinse with cold running water. Drain.

4. To serve, pour half of dressing into medium bowl. Add lettuce leaves and toss to coat. Line large platter with dressed lettuce leaves. Arrange potatoes, green beans, cherry tomatoes, tuna, hard-cooked eggs, and olives in separate piles on lettuce. Drizzle remaining dressing over salad.

EACH SERVING About 440 calories | 30 g protein | 30 g carbohydrate | 23 g total fat (4 g saturated) | 140 mg cholesterol | 716 mg sodium.

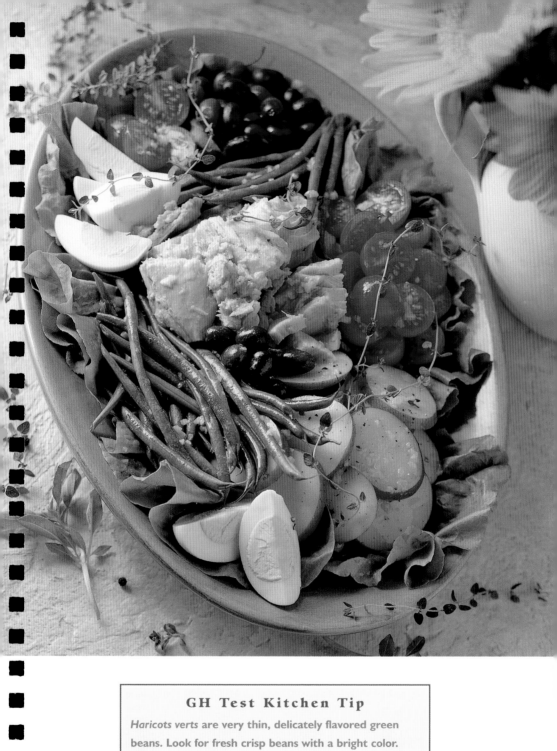

GH Test Kitchen Tip

Haricots verts are very thin, delicately flavored green
beans. Look for fresh crisp beans with a bright color.

Korean Steak in Lettuce Cups

Sliced round steak and shredded carrots are sautéed in a rich soy-ginger sauce and served in delicate Boston-lettuce leaves.

PREP 15 minutes   **COOK** 6 minutes   **MAKES** 4 main-dish servings

3 tablespoons soy sauce

1 tablespoon sugar

2 teaspoons Asian sesame oil

1 teaspoon minced, peeled fresh ginger

¼ teaspoon ground red pepper (cayenne)

1 garlic clove, crushed with garlic press

1 beef top round steak (about 1 pound), trimmed, cut into ½-inch cubes

4 celery stalks with leaves, thinly sliced

½ (10-ounce) package shredded carrots (1 ¾ cups)

3 green onions, thinly sliced

1 tablespoon sesame seeds

1 head Boston lettuce, separated into leaves

green-onion tops for garnish

1. In medium bowl, stir soy sauce, sugar, oil, ginger, ground red pepper, and garlic until blended. Add beef, turning to coat with soy-sauce mixture, and marinate 15 minutes at room temperature, stirring occasionally.

2. In nonstick 12-inch skillet, heat celery, carrots, and *⅓ cup water* to boiling over medium-high heat. Cook 2 to 3 minutes or until vegetables are tender-crisp, stirring occasionally. Add beef with its marinade and cook 2 minutes or until meat just loses its pink color throughout, stirring quickly and constantly. Stir in green onions and sesame seeds, and cook 1 minute, stirring.

3. To serve, let each person place some beef mixture on a lettuce leaf. Garnish with green-onion tops. If you like, fold sides of lettuce leaf over filling to make a package to eat out of hand.

EACH SERVING About 250 calories | 28 g protein | 12 g carbohydrate | 10 g total fat (3 g saturated) | 53 mg cholesterol | 855 mg sodium.

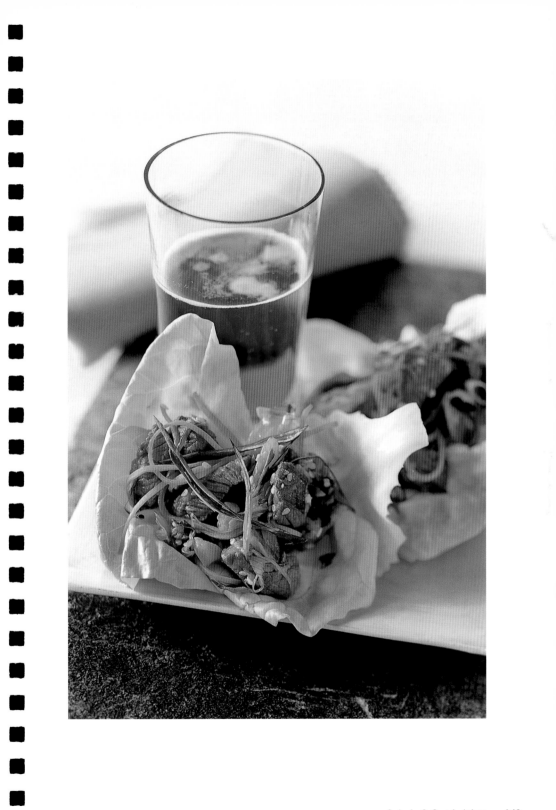

Beef and Pepper Fajitas

We seasoned a flank steak with a spicy rub before searing it in a grill pan for these tasty Mexican wraps.

PREP 30 minutes **COOK** 20 minutes **MAKES** 6 main-dish servings

2 limes

1 garlic clove, crushed with garlic press

2 tablespoons plus ¾ teaspoon chili powder

1 tablespoon plus ½ teaspoon brown sugar

¾ teaspoon salt

1 beef flank steak (about 1 pound), trimmed

2 teaspoons olive oil

1 large red pepper, thinly sliced

1 large green pepper, thinly sliced

1 large red onion, cut in half and thinly sliced

6 burrito-size flour tortillas, warmed

accompaniments: salsa, light sour cream, cilantro leaves (optional)

1. From limes, grate 1 teaspoon peel and squeeze 2 tablespoons plus 1 teaspoon juice.

2. In large bowl, mix garlic, lime peel, 2 tablespoons lime juice, 2 tablespoons chili powder, 1 tablespoon sugar, and ½ teaspoon salt until blended. Add steak to bowl and rub all over with chili-powder mixture. Marinate steak 15 minutes at room temperature or up to 1 hour in the refrigerator.

3. Heat grill pan over medium-high heat until hot. Add steak and cook 20 to 25 minutes for medium-rare or until of desired doneness, turning steak over once (reduce heat to medium if steak browns too quickly).

4. Meanwhile, in nonstick 12-inch skillet, heat oil over medium heat until hot. Add peppers and onion and cook covered, 10 minutes, stirring occasionally. Add remaining ¾ teaspoon chili powder, ½ teaspoon sugar, and ¼ teaspoon salt, and cook 5 minutes longer, uncovered, or until vegetables are tender and golden, stirring occasionally. Stir in remaining 1 teaspoon lime juice.

5. Transfer steak to cutting board; let stand 10 minutes to allow juices to set for easier slicing. Thinly slice steak and wrap in tortillas with pepper mixture. Serve with salsa, sour cream, and cilantro if you like.

EACH SERVING WITHOUT ACCOMPANIMENTS About 310 calories | **23 g protein** | **36g carbohydrate** | **9 g total fat (3 g saturated)** | **31 mg cholesterol** | **710 mg sodium.**

Philly Cheese Steaks

These sandwiches have all the flavor of the traditional Philadelphia treat but take half the time. To streamline prep, we broil the buns and beef while the onions and peppers cook on the stovetop.

 PREP 10 minutes   **COOK** 12 minutes   **MAKES** 4 sandwiches

1 teaspoon olive oil

1 jumbo onion (12 ounces), thinly sliced

1 medium red pepper, thinly sliced

1 medium green pepper, thinly sliced

4 hero-style rolls (about 3 ounces each), each cut horizontally in half

8 ounces thinly sliced deli roast beef

4 ounces thinly sliced Provolone cheese

1. In nonstick 12-inch skillet, heat olive oil over medium-high heat until hot. Add onion and peppers, and cook about 12 minutes or until tender and golden, stirring the mixture occasionally.

2. Meanwhile, preheat broiler. Place rolls, cut sides up, on rack in broiling pan. Top each bottom half with one-fourth of roast beef and one-fourth of cheese. With broiling pan 5 to 7 inches from source of heat, broil 1 to 2 minutes, until the cheese melts and the bread is toasted.

3. Pile onion mixture on top of melted cheese; replace top halves of rolls.

EACH SANDWICH About 620 calories | 35 g protein | 60 g carbohydrate | 26 g total fat (12 g saturated) | 94 mg cholesterol | 500 mg sodium.

Muffuletta

This savory meat and cheese sandwich with olives is a classic in the French Quarter of New Orleans, but with our recipe you won't have to travel to get it. The name comes from the Italian *muffuliette*, which refers to soft Sicilian rolls. The first muffuletta was served at Central Grocery Company, and serious sandwich fans claim it still serves the best.

PREP 30 minutes plus chilling   **MAKES** 8 main-dish servings

4 medium stalks celery, finely chopped (about 1¼ cups)

1 cup drained giardiniera (Italian mixed pickled vegetables), finely chopped

1 cup loosely packed fresh parsley leaves, chopped

¾ cup pitted green olives, finely chopped

¼ cup olive oil

¼ teaspoon coarsely ground black pepper

1 garlic clove, minced

1 round (10-inch-diameter) loaf soft French or Italian bread (1 pound), cut horizontally in half

6 ounces thinly sliced smoked ham

6 ounces thinly sliced provolone cheese

6 ounces thinly sliced Genoa salami

1. In medium bowl, combine celery, giardiniera, parsley, olives, oil, pepper, and garlic; set aside.

2. Remove a 1-inch layer of soft center of bread from both halves to make room for filling. On bottom half of bread, spread half of olive mixture; top with ham, cheese, salami, and remaining olive mixture. Replace top half of bread; press halves together.

3. Wrap sandwich tightly in plastic wrap, then foil, and refrigerate at least 2 hours or up to 24 hours. Cut into 8 wedges to serve.

EACH SERVING About 390 calories | 19 g protein | 26 g carbohydrate | 24 g total fat (8 g saturated) | 44 mg cholesterol | 1,515 mg sodium.

> ### GH Test Kitchen Tip
> The sandwich tastes even better when made a day ahead.

Chicken and Prosciutto Roll-Ups

This dish is easy to make but the presentation makes it a little special for a weekday meal. Serve with whole-grain bread.

PREP 10 minutes **COOK** 18 minutes **MAKES** 4 main-dish servings

4 medium skinless, boneless chicken-breast halves (about 1¼ pounds)

4 ounces Fontina cheese, cut into 4 slices

4 large slices prosciutto

12 large fresh basil leaves

1 bag (6 ounces) baby spinach

1. Holding knife parallel to work surface, cut a horizontal pocket in thickest part of each chicken breast. Insert 1 slice of cheese in each pocket.

2. Arrange prosciutto slices on work surface; top each with 3 basil leaves. Place a breast over each set of basil leaves; wrap with prosciutto to cover pocket. Secure with toothpicks.

3. Heat nonstick 12-inch skillet over medium heat until hot. Add chicken to skillet; cover and cook 10 minutes. Uncover; turn chicken over and cook 3 to 5 minutes longer or until chicken just loses its pink color throughout.

4. When chicken is done, place spinach in same skillet with chicken. Cook, uncovered, 1 minute or until leaves wilt, stirring constantly.

5. To serve, remove toothpicks from chicken. Arrange spinach on 4 dinner plates; top with chicken.

EACH SERVING About 305 calories | 45 g protein | 1 g carbohydrate, 13 g total fat (7 g saturated) | 125 mg cholesterol | 730 mg sodium.

Smoked Turkey and Mango Wraps

A sandwich of delightful counterpoints: luscious fresh mango—underscored by mango chutney—played against the rich meatiness of smoked turkey. The sandwich components are wrapped in lahvash, the soft version of Armenian cracker bread that ranges from 9 to 16 inches in diameter. Its thin texture is especially good with creamy spreads, like goat cheese or guacamole. If you can't find lahvash, divide filling ingredients among four 8- to 10-inch flour tortillas.

PREP 25 minutes plus chilling   **MAKES** 4 sandwiches

1 large lime

¼ cup light mayonnaise

3 tablespoons mango chutney, chopped

½ teaspoon curry powder

⅛ teaspoon paprika

1 lahvash (half 14-ounce package soft Armenian flatbread) (see Tip)

1 medium cucumber, peeled and thinly sliced

8 ounces thinly sliced smoked turkey breast

1 medium mango, peeled and finely chopped

6 large green-leaf lettuce leaves

1. Grate ¼ teaspoon peel and squeeze 1 tablespoon juice from lime. In small bowl, mix lime peel, lime juice, mayonnaise, chutney, curry, and paprika.

2. Unfold lahvash; spread with mayonnaise mixture. Top with cucumber slices, smoked turkey, chopped mango, and lettuce. Roll lahvash jelly-roll fashion.

GH Test Kitchen Tip

If lahvash seems dry before filling, place between dampened paper towels 10 to 15 minutes to soften.

---

3. Wrap lahvash roll in plastic and refrigerate 2 to 4 hours to allow bread to soften and flavor to develop.

4. To serve, trim ends, then cut lahvash roll into 4 pieces.

EACH SANDWICH About 280 calories | **18 g protein** | **51 g carbohydrate** | **2 g total fat (0 g saturated)** | **23 mg cholesterol** | **860 mg sodium.**

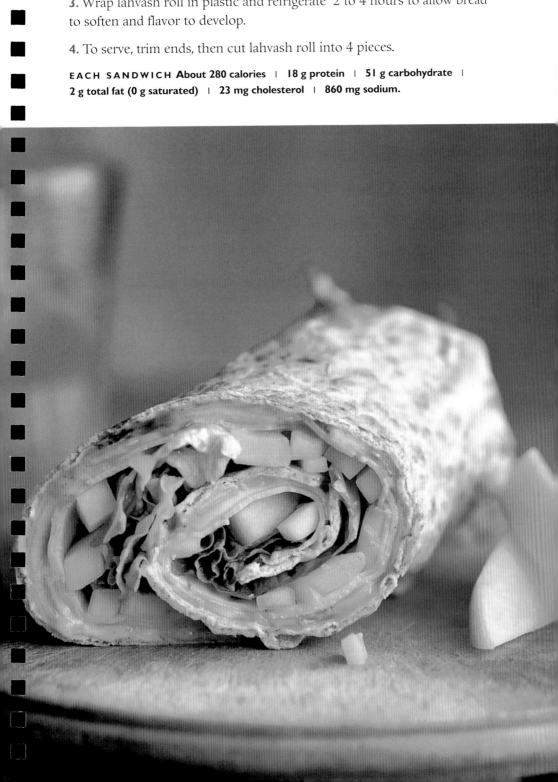

Spicy Guacamole and Chicken Roll-Ups

Chock-full of chicken and served warm, this hearty sandwich is sure to please. The zesty guacamole tastes great with tortilla chips, too.

PREP 30 minutes   **COOK** 12 minutes   **MAKES** 4 sandwiches

2 teaspoons olive oil

4 medium skinless, boneless chicken-breast halves (about 1 pound)

½ teaspoon salt

½ teaspoon coarsely ground black pepper

2 medium avocados (about 8 ounces each), peeled and cut into small chunks

1 medium tomato, diced

¼ cup loosely packed fresh cilantro leaves, coarsely chopped

4 teaspoons fresh lime juice

2 teaspoons finely chopped red onion

1 teaspoon adobo sauce from canned chipotle chiles (see Tip) or 2 tablespoons green jalapeño sauce

4 burrito-size (10-inch-diameter) flour tortillas, warmed

2 cups sliced iceberg lettuce

1. In 10-inch skillet, heat olive oil over medium-high heat until hot. Add chicken and sprinkle with ¼ teaspoon salt and ¼ teaspoon pepper. Cook chicken about 12 minutes, turning once, until juices run clear when thickest part is pierced with tip of knife. Transfer chicken to plate; cool 5 minutes or until easy to handle.

2. Meanwhile, in medium bowl, with rubber spatula, gently stir avocados, tomato, cilantro, lime juice, red onion, adobo sauce, and remaining ¼ teaspoon salt and ¼ teaspoon pepper until blended.

GH Test Kitchen Tip

Canned chipotle chiles in adobo (smoked jalapeño chiles in a vinegary marinade) are available in Hispanic markets and some large supermarkets.

---

3. Pull chicken into thin shreds. Place tortillas on work surface; spread with guacamole. Place chicken, then lettuce on top of guacamole. Roll tortillas around filling.

EACH SANDWICH About 510 calories | 34 g protein | 40 g carbohydrate | 25 g total fat (4 g saturated) | 72 mg cholesterol | 625 mg sodium.

Chicken Caesar Pockets

A sandwich and a salad rolled into one, these pockets make great picnic fare. Of course, you can always skip the pita and serve the salad on its own.

PREP 20 minutes   **COOK** 12 minutes   **MAKES** 6 sandwiches

¼ teaspoon salt

2 teaspoons plus 3 tablespoons olive oil

½ teaspoon coarsely ground black pepper

4 medium skinless, boneless chicken-breast halves (about 1 pound)

3 tablespoons lemon juice

3 tablespoons light mayonnaise

1 tablespoon Dijon mustard

1 teaspoon anchovy paste

1 small garlic clove, crushed with garlic press

½ cup grated Parmesan cheese

6 pitas (6- to 7-inch diameter)

8 cups sliced Romaine lettuce (about 12-ounce head)

1. Preheat broiler. In medium bowl, mix salt, 2 teaspoons olive oil, and ¼ teaspoon pepper. Add chicken and stir to coat. Place chicken on rack in broiling pan. Place pan in broiler at closest position to source of heat; broil chicken about 12 minutes, turning once, until juices run clear when thickest part is pierced with tip of knife. Transfer chicken to cutting board; cool 5 minutes or until chicken is easy to handle.

2. Meanwhile, in large bowl, with fork, mix lemon juice, mayonnaise, mustard, anchovy paste, garlic, remaining 3 tablespoons olive oil, and ¼ teaspoon pepper until blended; stir in Parmesan cheese.

3. With sharp knife, slit top third of each pita to form an opening. Thinly slice chicken. Add lettuce and chicken slices to dressing; toss well to coat. Fill pitas with salad.

EACH SANDWICH About 345 calories | 17 g protein | 39 g carbohydrate | 13 g total fat (3 g saturated) | 26 mg cholesterol | 770 mg sodium.

Tuscan Tuna on Focaccia

This filling also tastes great served in pita pockets. Be sure to rinse the cannellini beans—it removes some of the sodium.

🕑 **PREP** 15 minutes   **MAKES** 4 sandwiches

1 can (16 to 19 ounces) white kidney beans (cannellini), rinsed and drained

½ cup chopped fresh basil leaves

3 tablespoons capers, chopped

2 tablespoons fresh lemon juice

2 tablespoons olive oil

½ teaspoon salt

¼ teaspoon ground black pepper

1 can (6 ounces) tuna packed in water, drained

1 bunch watercress, trimmed

1 round or square (8-inch) focaccia bread, cut horizontally in half

2 ripe tomatoes, thinly sliced

1. In large bowl, mash 1 cup kidney beans. Stir in basil, capers, lemon juice, olive oil, salt, and pepper. Add tuna, watercress, and remaining beans; toss well.

2. Spoon tuna mixture on the bottom half of focaccia; top with tomato slices. Replace top of focaccia.

EACH SANDWICH About 490 calories | 32 g protein | 65 g carbohydrate | 13 g total fat (1 g saturated) | 7 mg cholesterol | 1,455 mg sodium.

Whole Wheat Pita Pizzas with Vegetables

We topped whole wheat pitas with ricotta cheese, garbanzo beans, and sautéed vegetables for a fast dinner the whole family will love.

PREP 25 minutes **BAKE** 10 minutes **MAKES** 4 main-dish servings

1 teaspoon olive oil

1 medium red onion, sliced

2 garlic cloves, crushed with garlic press

¼ teaspoon crushed red pepper

8 ounces broccoli flowerets (half 16-ounce bag), cut into 1 1/2-inch pieces

½ teaspoon salt

1 can (15 to 19 ounces) garbanzo beans, rinsed and drained

1 cup part-skim ricotta cheese

4 whole wheat pitas (6-inch diameter), split horizontally in half

½ cup grated Parmesan cheese

2 medium plum tomatoes, cut into ½-inch chunks

1. Preheat oven to 450°F. In nonstick 12-inch skillet, heat olive oil over medium-high heat until hot. Add onion and cook 7 to 10 minutes or until golden, stirring occasionally. Add garlic and crushed red pepper, and cook 30 seconds, stirring. Add broccoli flowerets, ¼ teaspoon salt, and ¼ *cup water*; heat to boiling. Reduce heat to medium and cook, covered, 5 minutes or until broccoli is tender-crisp.

2. Meanwhile, in small bowl, with potato masher or fork, mash beans with ricotta and remaining ¼ teaspoon salt until almost smooth.

3. Arrange pita halves on 2 large cookie sheets. Bake 3 minutes or until lightly toasted. Spread bean mixture on toasted pitas. Top with broccoli mixture and sprinkle with Parmesan. Bake 7 to 10 minutes longer or until heated through. Sprinkle with tomatoes to serve.

EACH SERVING About 510 calories | 27 g protein | 77 g carbohydrate | 13 g total fat (6 g saturated) | 27 mg cholesterol | 1,155 mg sodium.

Vegetarian Souvlaki

No one will miss the meat in these yummy sandwiches. Make the filling by cutting up your favorite veggie burgers.

PREP 15 minutes **COOK** 20 minutes **MAKES** 4 main-dish servings

1 tablespoon olive oil

1 large onion, cut in half and thinly sliced

4 frozen vegetarian soy burgers (10- to 12-ounce package), cut into 1-inch pieces

¼ teaspoon ground black pepper

½ teaspoon salt

8 ounces plain nonfat yogurt

8 ounces English (seedless) cucumber, cut into ¼-inch dice

1 teaspoon dried mint

1 small garlic clove, crushed with garlic press

4 pitas (6- to 7-inch diameter), warmed

1 medium tomato, cut into ½-inch dice

1 ounce feta cheese, crumbled

1. In nonstick 12-inch skillet, heat olive oil over medium heat until hot. Add onion and cook 12 to 15 minutes or until tender and golden, stirring occasionally. Add burgers, pepper, and ¼ teaspoon salt, and cook 5 minutes or until heated through.

2. Meanwhile, in medium bowl, stir yogurt with cucumber, mint, garlic, and remaining ¼ teaspoon salt. Add burger mixture and toss gently to combine.

3. Cut 1-inch slice from each pita to form an opening. Reserve cut-off pitas for crumbs another day. Spoon one-fourth burger mixture into each pita. Sprinkle with tomato and feta.

EACH SERVING About 390 calories | 24 g protein | 45 g carbohydrate | 13 g total fat (3 g saturated) | 9 mg cholesterol | 945 mg sodium.

Vegetarian Black-Bean Burritos

A deceptively rich and tasty combination of fat-free bean chili, rice, fresh corn, and spicy cheese—all wrapped up in warm flour tortillas.

PREP 10 minutes   **COOK** 15 minutes   **MAKES** 4 main-dish servings

½ cup regular long-grain rice

4 low-fat flour tortillas (10-inch diameter)

1¼ cups fresh corn kernels (about 2 large ears corn)

1 can (15 ounces) spicy fat-free black-bean chili

1 can (8 ounces) tomato sauce

¼ cup shredded Monterey Jack cheese with jalapeño chiles (1 ounce)

⅓ cup packed fresh cilantro leaves, chopped

1. Preheat oven to 300°F. In 2-quart saucepan, prepare rice as label directs but do not add salt or butter or margarine.

2. Meanwhile, wrap tortillas in foil; heat in oven until warm, about 15 minutes.

3. When rice is done, stir in corn, black-bean chili, and tomato sauce. Heat to boiling over medium-high heat; boil 1 minute.

4. Spoon about 1 cup chili mixture down center of each tortilla; sprinkle with cheese and cilantro. Fold sides of tortillas over filling. Place burritos seam side down on platter.

EACH SERVING About 430 calories | 15 g protein | 75 g carbohydrate | 8 g total fat (2 g saturated) | 8 mg cholesterol | 910 mg sodium.

Falafel Sandwiches

Serve these small bean patties in pita pockets with lettuce, tomatoes, and cucumbers. For a tangy finishing touch, spoon in a little plain yogurt (see photo on page 135).

PREP 10 minutes   **COOK** 8 minutes per batch   **MAKES** 4 sandwiches

4 green onions, cut into 1-inch pieces

2 garlic cloves, each cut in half

½ cup packed fresh Italian parsley leaves

2 teaspoons dried mint

1 can (15 to 19 ounces) garbanzo beans, rinsed and drained

½ cup plain dried bread crumbs

1 teaspoon ground coriander

1 teaspoon ground cumin

1 teaspoon baking powder

½ teaspoon salt

¼ teaspoon ground red pepper (cayenne)

¼ teaspoon ground allspice

olive oil nonstick cooking spray

4 pitas (6- to 7-inch diameter)

accompaniments: sliced romaine lettuce, sliced tomatoes, sliced cucumber, sliced red onion, plain low-fat yogurt

1. In food processor with knife blade attached, finely chop green onions, garlic, parsley, and mint. Add garbanzo beans, bread crumbs, coriander, cumin, baking powder, salt, ground red pepper, and allspice, and blend until a coarse puree forms.

2. Shape bean mixture, by scant ½ cups, into eight 3-inch round patties and place on sheet of waxed paper. Spray both sides of patties with olive oil spray.

3. Heat nonstick 10-inch skillet over medium-high heat until hot. Add half of patties and cook 8 minutes or until dark golden brown, turning once. Transfer the patties to paper towels to drain. Repeat with the remaining patties.

4. Cut off top third of each pita to form a pocket. Place warm patties in pitas. Serve with choice of accompaniments.

EACH SANDWICH WITHOUT ACCOMPANIMENTS About 365 calories |
14 g protein | 68 g carbohydrate | 5 g total fat (1 g saturated) |
0 mg cholesterol | 1,015 mg sodium.

Pinto-Bean Burgers

These zesty burgers are a family-friendly solution when you need to have dinner on the table fast.

🍳 **PREP** 15 minutes   **COOK** 8 minutes   **MAKES** 4 main-dish servings

1 can (15 to 15½ ounces) pinto beans, rinsed and drained

1 teaspoon ground cumin

1 teaspoon minced canned chipotle chile in adobo (see Tip, page 158)

1 slice pickled jalapeño chile, minced

2 tablespoons plus ½ cup mild salsa

5 tablespoons plain dried bread crumbs

2 tablespoons olive oil

4 hamburger buns, warmed

4 lettuce leaves

cilantro leaves, sliced red onion, and sour cream (optional)

1. In medium bowl, with potato masher, mash beans until almost smooth. Stir in cumin, chipotle, jalapeño, 2 tablespoons salsa, and 2 tablespoons bread crumbs until combined.

2. Place remaining 3 tablespoons bread crumbs on sheet of waxed paper. With floured hands, shape bean mixture into four 3-inch round burgers; coat with bread crumbs.

3. In nonstick 12-inch skillet, heat olive oil over medium heat until hot. Add burgers and cook about 8 minutes or until lightly browned on both sides and heated through, turning burgers over once halfway through cooking.

4. Spoon remaining ½ cup salsa on bottom halves of buns; top with lettuce and burgers. Serve burgers with cilantro, red onion, and sour cream if you like.

EACH SERVING About 350 calories | 11 g protein | 51 g carbohydrate | 11 g total fat (2 g saturated) | 0 mg cholesterol | 775 mg sodium.

Photography Credits

Index

Metric Conversion Chart

The recipes that appear in this cookbook use the standard United States method for measuring liquid and dry or solid ingredients (teaspoons, tablespoons, and cups). The information on this chart is provided to help cooks outside the U.S. successfully use these recipes. All equivalents are approximate.

METRIC EQUIVALENTS FOR DIFFERENT TYPES OF INGREDIENTS

A standard cup measure of a dry or solid ingredient will vary in weight depending on the type of ingredient. A standard cup of liquid is the same volume for any type of liquid. Use the following chart when converting standard cup measures to grams (weight) or milliliters (volume).

Standard Cup	Fine Powder (e.g., flour)	Grain (e.g., rice)	Granular (e.g., sugar)	Liquid Solids (e.g., butter)	Liquid (e.g., milk)
1	140 g	150 g	190 g	200 g	240 ml
3/4	105 g	113 g	143 g	150 g	180 ml
2/3	93 g	100 g	125 g	133 g	160 ml
1/2	70 g	75 g	95 g	100 g	120 ml
1/3	47 g	50 g	63 g	67 g	80 ml
1/4	35 g	38 g	48 g	50 g	60 ml
1/8	18 g	19 g	24 g	25 g	30 ml

USEFUL EQUIVALENTS FOR LIQUID INGREDIENTS BY VOLUME

1/4 tsp	=					1 ml
1/2 tsp	=					2 ml
1 tsp	=					5 ml
3 tsp	=	1 tbls	=		1/2 fl oz =	15 ml
		2 tbls	=	1/8 cup	1 fl oz =	30 ml
		4 tbls	=	1/4 cup	2 fl oz =	60 ml
		5 1/3 tbls	=	1/3 cup	3 fl oz =	80 ml
		8 tbls	=	1/2 cup	4 fl oz =	120 ml
		10 2/3 tbls	=	2/3 cup	5 fl oz =	160 ml
		12 tbls	=	3/4 cup	6 fl oz =	180 ml
		16 tbls	=	1 cup	8 fl oz =	240 ml
		1 pt	=	2 cups	16 fl oz =	480 ml
		1 qt	=	4 cups	32 fl oz =	960 ml
					33 fl oz =	1000 ml = 1

USEFUL EQUIVALENTS FOR DRY INGREDIENTS BY WEIGHT

(To convert ounces to grams, multiply the number of ounces by 30.)

1 oz	=	1/16 lb	=	30 g
4 oz	=	1/4 lb	=	120 g
8 oz	=	1/2 lb	=	240 g
12 oz	=	3/4 lb	=	360 g
16 oz	=	1 lb	=	480 g

USEFUL EQUIVALENTS FOR COOKING/OVEN TEMPERATURES

	Fahrenheit	Celsius	Gas Mark
Freeze Water	32° F	0° C	
Room Temperature	68° F	20° C	
Boil Water	212° F	100° C	
Bake	325° F	160° C	3
	350° F	180° C	4
	375° F	190° C	5
	400° F	200° C	6
	425° F	220° C	7
	450° F	230° C	8
Broil			Grill

USEFUL EQUIVALENTS FOR LENGTH

(To convert inches to centimeters, multiply the number of inches by 2.5.)

1 in	=		2.5 cm
6 in	=	1/2 ft =	15 cm
12 in	=	1 ft =	30 cm
36 in	=	3 ft = 1 yd =	90 cm
40 in	=		100 cm = 1 m